# Don't Get Trampled
# BY THE Moose!

foreword by **PAUL ORBERSON**

your survival
guide for a wild
economy

**Mark Burgess**
**Keith Henschen**

© 2009 burhgen publications
All rights reserved
burhgenpublications.com

ISBN-13: 978-0-9817474-0-8
ISBN-10: 0-9817474-0-x

Layout by Edward Binkham Associates, LLC · binkham.com
Interior moose artwork by Adam Malin · adammalingallery.com

# Don't Get Trampled by the Moose!

### first edition
copyright july 2009

## mark burgess
– and –
## keith henschen

burhgen ✴ publications
burhgenpublications.com

# contents

# foreword
## by Paul Orberson

I believe every red-blooded human being on planet earth wants to make a difference with their life. Network marketing allows men and women with little money or experience to be in business for themselves. That really is the dream most people have.

**Don't Get Trampled By the Moose** is an excellent tool of encouragement in a world that needs encouragement. Network marketing representatives and potential representatives all too often find themselves at the "end of the rope." I believe this book can help representatives hang in there until something good happens. This text makes it very clear; the only way to great success is through great failure!

The timing for this book couldn't have been better as the world economies are in a funk and many forecasters are predicting they will be at below trend growth for years to come. Network marketing flourishes in the economic environment we find ourselves, and this text is a must read for individuals who want to make a difference in their family's financial futures via network marketing (or direct selling).

Starting is great, but the world doesn't need one more flash and dash person–it's full of those! The world needs folks who will stick and stay until the job is finished! Mark and Keith show that positive thinking and positive action is the formula for a positive life. This is a powerful step-by-step guide to success and should be on everyone's reading list!

Paul Orberson

Founder and President,
Fortune Hi Tech Marketing

# acknowledgements

I could not thank all of the people that had a part in teaching me lessons throughout my lifetime. Sometimes lessons are difficult; sometimes they are learned more easily. We are, however, the sum total of all our experiences, both good and bad. I am grateful there is One who teaches with loving hands and patient mercy—Almighty God. All blessings come from Him! I thank Him for giving His Son, Jesus Christ to purchase my redemption. This is the greatest gift of all! I honor Him with this effort, and wish to honor Him with my life.

I would not be complete without my loving wife and best friend, who shares in my dreams and goals with the greatest excitement. She is my love and support, without which I could not move forward.

My children are a blessing, and though grown, have had less interaction with me than usual these many months. To them I say thank you! I love you more than you could know.

To my parents, brothers, and other family members who have been supportive all the way, thank you! Other friends have been helpful and supportive; to you all I say a hearty, "thanks!"

–Mark Burgess

---

To say I am thankful for what I have been given does not seem to justly convey my gratitude for all the blessings. I recognize the unseen hand of the Almighty God working in my life and guiding me every step of the way. I thank Him for providing all that was necessary for this book to be completed.

I am so grateful to God for my wife. Faithful to me when I was unable to devote to her the time she and my children deserved. I am thankful for her attitude of love and affection, supporting me in every decision. Without her devotion and support, this book would be much different.

I must say "thank you" to my parents who have supported me from the very beginning. And, to my extended family and friends who have offered more than just moral support all along, I am very grateful.

–Keith Henschen

# introduction

For decades the American economy enabled scores of people to generate large sums of money through commerce. After every recession, and even the depression of the 1930's, our economy regained its strength and vitality. As time progressed, our nation began to rely more on the transfer of technology and information as our source of revenue, and less on the production of real goods. This led to a dependency on foreign economies and their ability to sustain our level of consumption of these products.

Over time, our nation became more and more indebted to these countries. American citizens have developed a voracious appetite for consumable goods and services far surpassing their ability to pay for those purchases, leading to uncontrolled use of credit and overwhelming debt. This materialistic mentality overrode the common sense that once prevailed in the American people.

As a result, we find ourselves in a predicament characterized by lower wages, job losses, business closings and cutbacks, and an unpredictable economy. People are uneasy and fearful of things to come. Therapists and counselors are busier than ever, as many people believe that we are in a trend spiraling downward toward a lower standard of living.

There is hope. This hope lies in the actions of the individual. The ability of people to change the course of their future is the hallmark of the spirit of individualism that built America. However, sometimes this change of course brings with it uncertainty and risk.

The early American pioneers knew what it meant to survive in a hostile and unforgiving environment, yet they persevered through the difficult times to carve out a nation that has no equal in the modern world. They realized the importance of having dreams, and pursuing those dreams at the cost of personal conveniences and even life itself. It is this rugged individualism that must once again prevail in the turbulent economic times we now find ourselves.

The true entrepreneur moves forward in the face of uncertainty and risk because he knows what he wants in life. He understands it is a journey, not a destination, and readily chooses freedom over security. With this mindset, there is no limit to the change that can be produced, both in the lives of individuals, and in the economies of the world.

# part 1

## the moose

### *"our economy"*

# chapter 1

## what is the moose?

# chapter 1

# what is the moose?

S everal years ago, I was in Montana for my best friend's wedding. I was a groomsman, and the rehearsal dinner was at the home of the parents of the bride. They live in a beautiful log cabin in the foothills of the Rocky Mountains. Upon entering their home, I could not help but notice all of the trophy mounts hanging on the walls, the glass boxes displaying stuffed game birds, and bear rugs on the floor.

While I was there, I had the opportunity to speak with the father of the bride who had worked as a field guide for big game hunting trips throughout the United States. He told me story after story about hunting and leading hunts for bear, mountain lion, elk, wild boar and other big game. I will never forget one of the stories he told about a dentist he took on a hunting trip.

He described one of the most beautiful places I could ever imagine. He told of a lake up in Alaska where the water was cold and crystal clear, and the trees and grass around it were a lush green. The sky was a brilliant blue with a smattering of puffy clouds. This was just the type of place you would want to build a secluded log cabin: a place to get away from the world and relax.

He continued with his story by telling me about the dentist who had done very well in his business, and who, though he was not really a hunter, had the money to do most anything he wanted. A big game hunt in the mountains of Alaska had always been this man's dream. He wanted to bring home a trophy to hang above the fireplace for everyone to see.

So, here he was in the wilderness, with his rifle in hand and all his hunting gear strapped to his body like a soldier of fortune. Early that morning, as they set out for their destination, they saw a pack of wolves running a deer, and heard an elk bugling off in the distance. This place was teeming with wildlife, but they were here for just one thing. They were here for one of the biggest of the big game animals in North America–a moose.

> We have actually moved into another era, one of which we call a "Moose" economy.

A moose is the most sought after of all the big game animals in Alaska. A bull moose can tip the scales at over 1,500 pounds. They are not known for their easy going temperament and cordiality. A moose would just as soon grind a hunter into the ground as it would eat the grass from the shallows of the lake. Here was this dentist, in the middle of the wilderness, inexperienced and out for the adventure of a lifetime.

Later that afternoon, they found the place they thought would be best for spotting a moose. They took their positions, hiding in the brush, and started their moose calls. As they called and waited, a big bull appeared out of the undergrowth on the edge of the lake. He took a few steps out into the water, turned and stopped just short of facing the two hunters across the lake. As the moose stood in the waters, scanning the edge of the woods for the location of its next rival, the dentist raised his rifle in haste, and without the greatest of aim, fired a shot.

The bullet screamed through the air at over two thousand feet per second and hit the moose. In his excitement the dentist stood up, and against the advice of his guide, quickly made his way to a clearing on the edge of the lake. This captured the attention of the now injured bull moose, which immediately started charging his way across the shallow lake, straight for the dentist. Without thought of danger, the dentist again raised his rifle towards the moose. He fired four more shots, emptying his rifle, before killing the massive beast, which fell only a few feet from where he stood.

At this point in the story, I asked the bride's father where he was while all this took place. He told me he had positioned himself behind a large tree to protect himself from being trampled by the moose. I asked him why he did not run to the lake shore to help the dentist. His reply was simply, "How could I help him, if I got trampled by the moose as well?"

Many people, like the dentist, are hunting. They are hunting for some "thing" to protect them from a wild economy. We are accustomed to a "Bull" or "Bear" market, but it is much wilder than that today. No one knows where this economy is going to "come out of the woods." It is on such a wild and turbulent course that many people have difficulty identifying it as either Bull or Bear. What do we mean by this? We have actually moved into another era, one of which we call a "Moose" economy.

Encountering a moose in the wild is not something the average person normally has on his "bucket" list of things to do. Just like a moose, our present economy is proving to be very dangerous. No one really wants our economy to be as wild and unpredictable as it is; however, as the saying goes, "It is what it is." We must do the best we can with what we have. Though a moose is not impossible to track, it is known to be elusive. Likewise, in our economy today, most people fear what is going to happen because the end result is so unpredictable. They are unable to track the economy, much like the dentist was unable to track the moose without the guide.

The metaphors of a Bull and Bear market are derived from the motion each animal uses to attack an adversary. When the market is in an up-swing, it is like a bull that will thrust up with his horns. In a Bull market, there is typically investor confidence, which results in motivating investors to buy. This buying is in anticipation of future price increases for a positive return on investments called capital gains. People are making money and have confidence in the future of the economy as well as their financial stability. Not only are they making money, they are spending money as well.

When the market is on a downward trend, it is more like a bear that swipes down with its claws. A Bear market is created by a steady drop in the stock market over a period of time. This decline is a result of a lack of confidence in the economy causing investors to sell their stocks in an effort to prevent a loss of their investment.

In a Bear market, people are less likely to make unnecessary expenditures. They begin "tightening the belt" on regular expenses and planning more carefully their vacations and family activities. Money is more carefully guarded because it is more difficult to obtain. People spend less, and businesses make less profit, resulting in financial stress in the economy. In some cases, an extended Bear market results in job losses and companies closing their doors.

Many characteristics of our economy are strikingly similar to the characteristics of a moose. When a moose charges, it has both characteristics of the bull and the bear. Upon initial contact with an opponent, a moose will, like a bull, drive upward with its antlers in an attempt to dislodge the adversary from his footing. Once the opponent is displaced, the moose will follow with a downward, stomping motion, in an attempt to crush the victim.

A Moose market is one in which confidence and security in the market swing wildly from one point to another, seemingly in no clearly traceable order or direction. There are no definable trends in a Moose economy. The only thing that is consistent in a Moose economy is change. These changes occur rapidly and without discretion. Therefore, the definition of a Moose economy is an economy in which unforeseeable financial events result in unstable and unpredictable swings in the stock market, rendering normal economic indicators useless for the average person.

In October of 2007 Democrats pushed for, and passed, the Affordable Housing Trust Fund Act while, on the other hand, Republicans were pushing to keep financial institutions from being regulated. It is proposed that these two actions did much to set in motion the course of events that led to the financial crisis our country faces today.

Along with other acts of Congress, the Affordable Housing Trust Fund Act inundated the market with an overabundance of money. This money was made available to borrowers at a low interest rate. The lax regulations on lending agencies allowed unqualified borrowers to receive loans for new homes. This rash of poor judgment on the part of lenders and borrowers led to a building boom. These high-risk homeowners eventually defaulted on their monthly mortgage payments, resulting in revenue loss in the banking system.

Financial institutions devised products containing multiple mortgage notes that hid the risks of the bad mortgages. These products were bought and sold between various financial institutions. The sale of these products allowed each party to make a profit while thinking they were passing the risk down the line. Ultimately, the risk landed on the federal government which resulted in private profits paid to the financial institution executives and socialized risk carried by the taxpayers.

Multitudes of people have already been trampled by the Moose economy in the form of foreclosures, bankruptcies, business closures and job losses. We have seen unprecedented deflation fears, capital losses, and bailouts. There have also been temporary upward swings with lower gas prices, spikes in stock market values, and lower prices brought on by deflation. Though deflation brings prices down, many times people will wait for prices to bottom before they purchase, making it harder for businesses to stay afloat. The results of these circumstances give further credibility to the concept of an unpredictable Moose economy.

> Many characteristics of our economy are strikingly similar to the characteristics of a moose.

The Moose economy carries with it different implications to different groups of people. For those who are in the baby boomer generation, the retirement funds and stocks in which they so heavily invested have abruptly declined in value. This decline forced many to rethink retirement and some to even rejoin the workforce. Generations X and Y are finding themselves questioning the dogma instilled in them as children.

There is no longer safety and security in a job. Many people have recognized that their college degree no longer holds the advantage it once did. With news of the possible collapse of the Social Security system, Americans are learning to depend on themselves for their financial future, not a corporation or the government.

Lack of education is one of the main reasons so many people are in financial bondage. The Federal Government, which took over the responsibility of educating our children decades ago, has failed to educate every student in proper fundamental principles concerning banking, credit, budgeting, and economics. Parents have also failed to teach their children these basic and essential elements of finance. Many students graduate from high school without understanding how to manage personal finances, how to write a resume, or what an employer looks for in an employee. They also have no knowledge of how our government works, or the basic history of our nation.

These are only a few of the basic subjects students should understand to make the simplest financial decisions. The failure to educate our students in finance is evidenced in the rising number of bankruptcies and foreclosures. Scores of people are finding themselves over-extended on their credit. As early as thirty years ago, there were segments of the American population who shunned the idea of credit. There are stories of those who carried a line of credit with a local merchant, who were looked down upon because they were too poor to pay for their purchases in cash.

> Multitudes of people have already been trampled by the Moose economy in the form of foreclosures, bankruptcies, business closures and job losses.

As time progressed and our world became smaller, credit cards were introduced for the safety and convenience of the traveling salesman. The idea of credit cards rapidly grew popular when more people realized their convenience and began using them as well. People who paid with credit, because they did not have the cash, became more accepted. The number of people using credit simply camouflaged the number of people who could not afford the purchases.

As Americans grew more accustomed to buying with credit, the concept of living without debt became more foreign. Generations X and Y grew up believing money came from a card, and when they received their first credit card, they treated it as though it were free money. They started using it for anything and everything they wanted, not realizing the consequences that would follow.

Multitudes of adults, young and old alike, are finding themselves with nothing to show for their years of hard work. Although they consider themselves to be fairly responsible with their money, they have failed to learn about personal finance. Some feel it is a daily struggle just to make ends meet. They are so far behind they feel they may never catch up, much less get ahead financially.

It is important for a person who is looking for a way to hedge against a wild economy to find the right guide to help them through troubled times. The dentist was very successful in his expertise, which was fixing someone's smile, but had no clue when it came to hunting. He may have known how to load, aim, and even fire his rifle, but when it came to tracking a moose, finding the best spot for the hunt, calling the moose, and patiently waiting for the right moment, he needed a guide to help him.

> It is important for a person who is looking for a way to hedge against a wild economy to find the right guide to help them through troubled times.

There are people who understand current conditions, and have found a solution for the wild economy. However, the majority of people are unsuspecting, uneducated, or just apathetic. The average person is blindly feeling his way on a crash course destined to be trampled by the moose.

As humans, we are often so captivated and enamored with what others do and have that we will do anything to achieve the same. People who are motivated by external values often jump head long into the first thing presented to them that offers promise of a better future. We are bombarded daily with ads claiming to be the best opportunity to build wealth. In the past, many of these have turned out to be scams and schemes brewed up by dishonest money-grubbers. There are many legitimate business opportunities available which produce fantastic sums of money for those who work them.

Many people refuse to entertain the idea of looking at these opportunities because they think they are illegitimate. The fact is, no business is illegitimate as long as it works for you. Each individual must decide for himself what is best for him. The only criteria for the right kind of business opportunity should be that it does not cross any legal, ethical or moral boundaries.

You must realize there is not a "one size fits all" solution for financial self-reliance, and that there is value in having a "guide" to help you through the maze of options. The only reason the dentist survived was because he kept shooting. He did not give up. You must have the same attitude to prevent being trampled by the moose.

# chapter 2

## the new horizon

# chapter 2

# the new horizon

In business, as in life, if you cannot see the big picture you will have difficulty achieving personal and financial success. Without a vision of the big picture, you will only ever have a limited view of where you have been, where you are now, and where you could be. This is why the wealthy see things before they happen while the poor see them after they happen.

The ability to see the end of something from the beginning is a critical element of success. It is the difference between standing at the top of the Grand Canyon looking down at a raft on the river, or being in the raft. For example, when the "Dot Com" craze hit the marketplace, there were those who looked at the opportunity from above, saw the potential and made millions. There were others who looked at it from the viewpoint of the raft, not realizing what happened until too late, and consequently earned little.

A similar case occurred with the creation of the Microsoft Corporation. Bill Gates saw from the beginning what the operating system "DOS" would do for the computer industry, and as a result, became one of the richest men in history. This foresight allows a person to make the proper choices that will lead them to success.

You also have the unique opportunity to see something before it takes place. At this time in history, people are realizing the fallacy in the idea of becoming wealthy or financially independent by working for someone else. They are also beginning to understand that hard work alone is not the answer, but becoming business owners and working hard for themselves is the key to their financial freedom. This reality is creating the beginning of a grand movement like never before, a movement where people are fleeing toward home-based businesses at an unprecedented pace.

> The ability to see the end of something from the beginning is a critical element of success.

When our nation was in its infancy, the majority of people were business owners. Those businesses may not fit our strict definition of a business today with balance sheets, share holder reports and a company prospectus, but people traded for goods and services on a personal level. They knew the value of certain commodities and how to live within a budget. They were able to survive with what they could raise on the farm, hunt in the woods, or create with their hands. They took advantage of whatever market worked for them.

For the majority of the twentieth century, the era of the corporation was strong and thriving. People felt secure in this environment. Large companies were the answer to the "American dream" because they were able to offer more secure jobs and better benefits than one could obtain as a small business owner. These benefits helped to lure people out of the self-reliance era into the dependence-on-a-company era.

Today, large companies are still employing people, but they are reducing their overhead by cutting jobs and reducing their operations on a wide scale. Many employees now have an overwhelming sense of insecurity in working for someone else. They are tired of how they are being treated by big business, and no longer is the corporation the answer.

As corporations continue to cut jobs and lay off employees, there are two expanding groups of people in our society, the first of which are those who are deep in debt. According to Experian, the national credit scoring agency, the average person carries a consumer debt of $16,635. (*U.S. News and World Report*, "The End of Credit Card Consumerism,"

August 2008.) Many of these people are quickly approaching the end of their rope financially.

The second group is those who are staying afloat financially, but want or feel they deserve more out of life. These individuals are often employees who have what most people consider a steady job. They realize they are only breaking even each month, with just enough money to go out to eat or occasionally catch a movie.

We are witnessing the beginning of a paradigm shift in how people view their source of income. People are looking for a better solution not only to become financially independent, but in many cases, just to survive financially. Fear and uncertainty in the economy are causing them to reevaluate their attitude of spending versus saving. This has led many people to search for additional sources of income.

> They [people] are not only looking for financial freedom, they are looking for personal freedom.

Many are beginning to understand that the only way to produce positive financial change is to decrease spending, to increase income, or both. Whether they are mowing lawns, trimming shrubs or working a part time job at the local diner, depending on their situation, they are making an effort either to make ends meet or to get ahead.

Once again people are realizing the value in owning a small or home-based business. They are not only looking for financial freedom, they are looking for personal freedom. While we know we cannot control everything, there are things we can control. We understand we cannot control the moose in the woods, but we are able to prepare for an encounter with the moose. We cannot control prices, inflation, or the economy, but we can control our income and spending. We must take responsibility for our actions, in spite of the decisions politicians make that negatively influence the economy.

Many people believe there is a "science" to building wealth. Just as there are laws in nature, there are principles of wealth that remain the same regardless of the circumstances. If you understand and employ these principles, you can build wealth in any economic situation.

It does not take a rocket scientist to understand the concept: to have more you must do more. If you are working fifty to sixty hours per week already, it is very difficult to do any more, unless you are of the opinion that eating and sleeping are highly overrated. One of the best ways to accomplish this is to become a business owner.

There are those who have, for many years, produced their income in a home-based business. They are the true mavericks in this trend. These people have blazed a trail for others to follow, and many *are* following. Companies with a sound business plan and strong leadership who cater to this segment of our society will, in the near future, see unprecedented growth.

> It does not take a rocket scientist to understand the concept: to have more you must do more.

Many people do not believe they have what it takes to own and operate a business. For some, this is true, but for many more, it is a matter of conditioning. We, as Americans, are taught to get a degree so we can get a "good job." Therefore, business ownership is not something we have been conditioned to believe we can do.

The good news is that there are more opportunities available today than ever before to own a business. Just the tax incentives alone are motivation enough for having a home-based business. In recent months, poor economic choices have been made that affect not only our nation, but the world. When government officials, bankers and businessmen make decisions with only the immediate results in mind, they affect the future economy in a very negative way. We can only hope our elected officials see the value of keeping these tax breaks for home-based business owners.

It is essential for a business to have a commerce friendly environment in order to achieve the goals of the owner. Business owners help make our economy successful by producing job opportunities for individuals and by generating tax revenues for the central government. Since business equals jobs, everything possible should be done to help business owners, not hinder them.

There are government officials that have seemingly made it their mission to reverse the ideals of capitalism in an effort to bring about a socialistic society. The motivation for socialism has always been to eliminate the so-called disparity between the social classes. History has proven that the experiment of socialism has failed every time it has been tried.

There will always be a lower, middle and upper class in society because of those who are satisfied with the status quo. The distinction between economic classes of people exists because there is a group of people who will never own a business. This means there will always be those who only know how to follow, mainly because they are comfortable in their current position as laborers.

Historically, those who were leaders were often wealthy. We read stories about men and women born into the middle or lower class, and because of their leadership skills, became wealthy and moved into the upper class. The same can be said for some who were born into the upper class who were lacking those same skills. They lost everything, only to find themselves homeless and depraved.

Not everyone has the personality or ability to lead others. There are individuals who will never become business owners. Yet, in such a wild economy, it is still imperative to prepare for the moose encounter. This preparation will require most people to somehow increase their income. For many, the answer to this quandary is to become a business owner. There are several ways for the person with the ambition to start and run a business to accomplish this. He can start or purchase what is called a brick and mortar business. This is generally a conventional business where he will own or rent a building, stock inventory, and produce, and/or sell a product or service.

> History has proven that the experiment of socialism has failed every time it is tried.

A person can also start a business using the internet as his storefront. Internet businesses typically market a product line to consumers via a website. With this business, the overhead is much lower than a conventional business and often inventory can be managed through drop shipping.

An increasingly popular way to build a substantial income is to become a representative of a network marketing company. Like internet marketing, network marketing has low overhead. It often involves marketing a product or service and building an organization of independent representatives.

Those who start a business should select carefully the vehicle that will carry them through the rough times as well as the good. If a person lacks the knowledge and resources to start a business, he should at least champion those who do.

# part 2

## the method

### *the solution to the moose economy*

# chapter 3

## benefits of a
## home-based business

**chapter 3**

# benefits of a
# home-based business

There is a distinction that must be drawn between home-based and conventional businesses. The biggest difference is that a conventional business involves a tangible building that is either rented or owned while a home-based business uses a part of the home. There are several great advantages to having a home-based business, taxes being one of them. Tax benefits apply to all businesses across the board. There are more than 150 tax benefits available to business owners that do not apply to employees.

An employee is taxed on his wages while a small business owner pays taxes on his profits. This means that before Dan the employee sees the first penny of his paycheck, Uncle Sam extracts the percentage dictated by his tax bracket. The remainder is what Dan is left with to pay for his mortgage, put gas in his car, purchase food for his family, pay whatever bills he may have, and hopefully have enough left to go see a movie.

On the other hand, John the small business owner pays his bills and covers his expenses, then pays taxes on what is not claimed as a deduction (his profits). John gets a deduction for his vehicle, his home office, his health care costs, and a plethora of other things of which Dan could only dream. The only thing the IRS requires to be considered a business is the intent of making a profit, good business records, and the dedication of working a minimum of three to four hours per week.

Personal freedom is one of the most exciting aspects of owning a business because it enables you to take control of your life. A home-based business can provide you with the ability to work at your own pace and on your own time. Since you do not punch a clock or report to work, you have the freedom to do what you want, when you want.

> Personal freedom is one of the most exciting aspects of owning a business because it enables you to take control of your life.

This freedom also gives you more time for your family. Working from home gives you time to build relationships with your children and spouse. Often, family members may help you accomplish more and increase your potential income.

Your earnings are not confined to a salary or tied to the number of hours you work. As a business owner, you are paid according to your performance. This fact alone is enough motivation for many to work harder and increase their productivity. If you are working your business while holding a job as an employee, you may simply see the benefit of extra cash flow to help pay the bills or save for a vacation or retirement.

With a home-based business, commute time is virtually eliminated. Now, instead of driving fifteen miles and sitting in traffic for forty-five minutes, you are walking fifteen steps to your home office and the only thing you are waiting for is your cup of coffee to finish brewing. A home office is much cheaper to maintain than a rented office on Main Street.

In many cases home-based business owners choose a line of work that complements their passion. This makes working enjoyable, and many who enjoy what they do forget about the time and work more hours. These business owners also experience less stress because they have an outlet for their creativity. The new shorter commute, the lower overhead costs, and augmented work time often translate to increased productivity which leads to increased income.

Although many people start a home-based business in the area of their expertise, this is not always necessary. There are many great opportunities available to those who do not have prior experience. There are publications available through your local book store and the internet that will provide information and ideas about owning a home-based business.

Many home-based businesses do not require employees. Having managed both union and non-union businesses, I can tell you this is very appealing. Having no employees means not only that you have the absence of the headaches that accompany your dependence on others to protect your business, but also that you do not have to share the revenues.

There are always two sides to any coin, so I must say that there are times when a home-based business can produce more revenue by leveraging the time of others. If this is the case for your business, you might want to consider the advantages of using family members, such as your spouse and children, to accomplish the necessary tasks. Utilizing family members can actually benefit you because salaries are an expense to the company and are, therefore, a tax benefit that keeps the flow of revenue within your home.

> A home-based business does not a guarantee that you will always have an income, but it places your financial future in your hands rather than in someone else's.

Home-based businesses do not have the limitations of territories. You have the freedom to advertise and market your products and services wherever you choose. This gives you the flexibility to move your business to another state if you so desire. Along these same lines is that some home-based businesses lend themselves well to working the business from anywhere. This means you can take longer trips with the family whenever you desire and still keep in touch with the necessities of your business.

One of the obvious reasons for owning a home-based business is the freedom from worry of being laid off from a job. This strikes a chord with many people around the country today. Having experienced this myself, it is a terrible thing to invest many years in a company and suddenly lose your income and the feeling of a secure future. A home-based business does not a guarantee that you will always have an income, but it places your financial future in your hands rather than in someone else's.

Because you are in control of your business and your future, owning a home-based business gives you the opportunity to expand and grow your business as you see fit. Your ideas and dreams are not limited by someone above you who does not share your vision. You have the potential for unlimited growth and prosperity within the actions that are generated by your dreams. The only limits are those you place upon yourself. Instead of working 30 years for a $300 watch, with the right home-based business, you may be able to work 36 months for 30+ years of freedom. The choice is yours.

# chapter 4

## the importance and value of time

# chapter 4

# the importance and value of time

It was closing in on the Christmas holiday, and I was at home watching television. One of the stations was airing a series of Christmas movies leading up to Christmas day. The movie for that evening was Charlie and the Chocolate Factory starring Johnny Depp.

I remember a scene in the movie where Charlie, the son of a poor factory worker, was looking for the last golden ticket to visit the chocolate factory. He is walking down the street when he finds a dollar bill. With excitement, he runs around the corner and into the candy store where he purchases a chocolate bar, which of course contains the last golden ticket. He runs home and shows his parents and grandparents who immediately begin to celebrate.

Amidst their jubilation, Charlie stops them to announce he is not going to the factory. He tells them he is going to sell the ticket to pay for the much needed repairs to their home and to purchase the food they need to get them through the winter. At that point Charlie's grandfather calls him to his bedside and tells him "Charlie, don't sell that ticket. There is plenty of money in the world, but what you have is a very limited commodity. They print more money every day."

We can learn a very valuable lesson from what Charlie's grandfather told him. We all possess a very limited commodity, and yet the majority of us sell it every day. What is that limited commodity? Time. A large percentage of Americans trade their time for money. They punch a clock to pay their bills. Why? Because most people either do not know how, or choose not to do anything different.

Most people live in what seems to be a vortex of life's ever busying affairs. As if we do not already have enough to do, we somehow find one more thing to add to our already packed daily agenda. Our society has invented countless devices to "save" time, which gives us an extra couple of minutes only to fill with yet another task.

> A large percentage of Americans trade their time for money. Time is so important because it is one of the only things in life we cannot replace.

It is imperative that each of us realize the importance of making the most of every hour we have been given. Stories are told of people whose perspective on life changed after seeing their whole life flash before their eyes in a situation where they faced eminent death. There are other stories of how near-death experiences have changed people in such dramatic ways that they quit their job to pursued the things they always wanted.

When you begin to grasp the brevity of life, the matter of time takes on a whole new meaning. Time is so important because it is one of the only things in life we cannot replace. Therefore, we must use it wisely. You must strive to get the most out of your time. The best way to accomplish this is by planning. In planning the activities of your day, you must evaluate each action to determine whether or not it is helping you reach your desired goals. Activities which are not beneficial to this end can then be removed from the schedule.

This is not to say activities with the family and hobbies are not allowed. Family time and recreation are vital to keeping the right perspective in everything you do. As the saying goes, "All work and no play makes Jack a dull boy." There must be a balance in your life that allows for leisure and times of renewal. Problems arise when people have too much recreation and entertainment as a part of their daily routine. This lack of balance creates the apathy that is prevalent in today's society.

Once you have examined your activities and made a plan, it must be implemented. This plan may change from time to time, but great value is derived from having and carrying out planned activities. This controls what is accomplished in a given day and keeps the unused and wasted time to a minimum.

If a business owner does not understand the value of his time, he will not use it wisely. Everyone determines the value of their time by the amount of money they are willing to trade for it. For example, if the person employed at the local manufacturing plant agrees to work for $15 an hour, to him, his time is worth only $15 per hour.

> The more valuable a person perceives his time to be worth, the more he will protect it and use it wisely.

People who trade their time for money often accept what is called "the going rate." This kind of thinking robs people of their independence. They feel they cannot do any better than what they are paid by an employer. Thus they become dependent on the employer, when in reality, there is *no* security in working for someone else.

Much of this mentality stems from the perspective of those who have a limited education or skill set. This mind-set, coupled with the law of supply and demand, causes most laborers to accept working for hourly wages. A demand greater than the supply of any given commodity raises its perceived and real value. A physician may earn around $95 per hour because his time is in higher demand due to few people possessing his skill and education.

Assuming you are one of the people mentioned in the previous paragraphs, you earn somewhere between $15 and $95 per hour. The only time you make money is when you are working. When you leave work, your pay stops until you go back to work the next day. Your pay is limited by the number of hours you work. Even if you worked every hour of the day, you could only make a limited amount of money because there are only twenty four hours in a day.

The more valuable a person perceives his time, the more he will protect it and use it wisely. We all have the same amount of time in a day. However, we do not all have the same number of days in which to accomplish our goals and dreams. Therefore, you must determine what your time is worth to you. To determine the desired value of your time, simply decide how much money you want to make, and divide this number by the total hours you are willing to work. It will look something like this: $200,000 a year income divided by 40 work hours per week equals $96.15 per hour.

When considering a business venture, you must remember your time is the most valuable asset you have. Time is actually more significant than money. You can always earn more money, but once time is gone, there is no replacing it. Therefore, you should set a bar at the value of what your time is worth. Once you reach that bar, you should reset it even higher. You will learn that, as a business owner, you are a leader. As such, you will be expected to "raise the bar" for those around you. Set the bar high, but within reason. Make your goals very specific, because "he who aims at nothing will hit it every time."

# chapter 5

## leverage

# chapter 5

# leverage

George is one of the hardest working business owners I know. He is constantly busy; sun up to sun down, George has a full schedule and is always on the move. Yet, George has one problem he cannot seem to overcome. As busy as he is, he is always broke.

He is not overspending; he pays his bills and lives in a small house, drives an older model vehicle, and rarely goes out to eat. He has a good customer base for his business. On average, he responds to about four calls a day and has virtually no unsatisfied customers. He charges a premium for his service because he provides only the best.

What George does not understand is the value of his time. His schedule is filled with insignificant interruptions that consume several hours of every day. Many home-based business owners struggle not only with managing their activities and making the most of their time, but using their time and assets to their advantage. As a business owner, the object is to make money. If you have distractions and trivial activities filling your schedule, you are not capitalizing on the full potential of your income.

George is lacking a quality that is very important as a business owner. It is a principle that can make the difference between one or more zeros at the end of his monthly bank statements. This principle is called leverage.

Leverage is utilizing the resources of people, time, money, influence, or any other asset to increase the potential of the outcome. Leverage is the key to working less and making more. John Paul Getty explained the practice of leverage when he said, "I'd rather have one percent of a hundred people's efforts than a hundred percent of my own." The key to leverage is to understand its value and be intentional in its implementation.

I will refer again to the physician and the factory worker. The physician is earning $95 per hour only when he is working. When he goes home or is on vacation, his income stops. A business owner, on the other hand, has the ability to earn an income from the labor of other people.

> Leverage is the key to working less and making more.

Business owners utilize leverage every day their employees show up for work. Because the business owner can employ others who are producing revenue for his company, he can still produce an income, even when he is away. The employee never receives all the revenue produced by his labor, yet he agrees to work for lesser wages. Why? Because the employer provides something for the employee that the employee cannot provide for himself–the perceived security of a job.

The employer deserves to make money from the employee's labor, because the employer provides not only the job, but oftentimes insurance and a retirement savings program among other things. In this relationship, the employer is usually more financially successful for one simple reason–leverage.

To truly leverage your time, you must not only earn an income while you are working, but also when you are not working. While you are working, the value of your time is higher. When you are not working, the amount of money earned is dependent upon the mechanisms or processes you have in place producing revenue. As these mechanisms and processes become more automated, they also become more valuable.

Leveraging personal time can be accomplished by having a meeting with five people at once rather than meeting five times with separate individuals. As a business owner, you should capitalize on this concept in as many activities as you possibly can. Any time you are able to perform a task one time and be in a position to reap the benefit and reward multiple times, you are in essence leveraging your time.

Leveraging the time of others occurs when you are able to duplicate your actions in someone else and reap a reward from their labors. For example, if Sally is a business owner and she hires Anita and Chris, Sally can leverage their time by training them to duplicate what she is doing. As they are working, Sally is earning a little from the labors of each. This is one of the ways being a business owner allows you to leverage the time of other people.

Leveraging can also include making money work for you. Whether it is your money or other people's money, it can be leveraged to produce more. As a business owner one way you can leverage your money is by purchasing products at wholesale and selling them retail.

Banks utilize this principle through what is called compound interest. Bankers lend money to an individual in return for the repayment of the balance of the loan plus a predetermined fee–the interest. Investors employ this same concept with their money, sometimes even through a bank.

Most business owners do not consider themselves to be a bank or lending agency, let alone an investor. When in reality, as someone decides to start his own business, he does, in fact, become

> To truly leverage your time, you must not only earn an income while you are working, but also when you are not working.

an investor. He invests in himself, his future, and the future of his family. He chooses to place a dollar amount on the table in return for the opportunity to make his money back many times over using the business model of his choice. Not only that, but when he becomes successful and produces an income greater than his expenses, he has the option to become an investor in other avenues, thereby leveraging his money.

Influence can also be leveraged. Every business owner has influence. That influence can be used to control the outcome of certain situations. Also, by aligning yourself with other businesses and business owners, you are able to expand your influence by leveraging theirs.

It is human nature to respect the accomplishments and positions of others. A corporate executive is able to walk into a meeting and negotiate a deal for his company because he carries with him a certain level of influence. The successful business owner is able also to leverage his influence to encourage others. When an individual sees and understands the prosperity of a successful home-based business owner, it can have an influence on his decision of whether or not to become one himself.

> The idea driving leverage is always to get more done by utilizing your assets to gain the strategic advantage, therefore increasing your potential outcome.

The idea driving leverage is always to get more done by utilizing your assets to gain the strategic advantage, therefore increasing your potential outcome. One benefit many overlook is the synergy generated by building an organization of people who are focused on a common goal. Business owners leverage employees, churches leverage church members, governments leverage citizens. This is not a negative thing, but rather very positive. When the work that needs to be done can be accomplished much quicker by leveraging people, it is only wise to utilize the efforts of everyone in the organization.

When understood completely, the advantages of leverage are too strong to be ignored. With leverage, you as a business owner are able to build a bigger business, build your business faster, and make more money. Leverage allows you to get more done, influence more people, and obtain stronger negotiating positions. Without leverage, you are simply an employee of the business you own.

# chapter 6

## multiple streams of profit

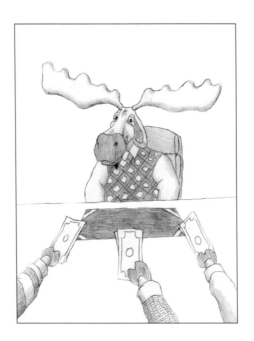

# chapter 6

# multiple streams of profit

Besides leveraging, you must understand and utilize this concept of multiple streams of profit. Many people trust their financial future to the one job they are devoted to working forty hours per week. They work hard and are loyal to their job as an employee or their business as a business owner. As they work, they are dependent on one source of income. Surely there is nothing wrong with that; "that is how dad always did it," right?

In times past, the issue of increasing your income was resolved by working a few more hours, or picking up a few extra jobs on the side. You could simply put in some overtime hours, and wow, what a difference in the paycheck. Do some handy work for a friend, and you had enough cash for two weeks spending money. Times have changed. Twenty dollars does not go as far as it once did and since companies are cutting hours, overtime is now out of the question for most.

Multiple streams of income refers to revenue generated from several unrelated sources. The benefit of this diversity is the income security provided if a product or service slows or fails. You are more likely to succeed with more than one source of revenue, because the loss of one does not mean the loss of all.

Having multiple streams of income is a strategy that enables the average person to create a better future for himself and his family. This is key to financial security because inevitably, economies change. When the market swings, if you have all your financial eggs in one basket, you may find yourself with a basket full of broken eggs.

For example, Frank has heavily invested in the housing market. He is a real estate agent who also owns a few properties he is trying to flip. Suddenly, the mortgage industry begins to flounder, resulting in the failure of mortgage companies. It becomes increasingly difficult to get a loan because mortgage companies have tightened regulations.

> The concept of multiple streams of income is widely accepted as a key principle in building wealth.

This impacts Frank because if loans are not available, he cannot sell any houses, resulting in a loss of income. If he loses his income, he cannot pay for loans of the houses he plans to resell. Frank soon files for bankruptcy because he had only one type of income. Had Frank understood the principle of multiple streams of income, he would have sold houses and, at the same time, been part of another type of industry not tied to real estate.

The concept of multiple streams of income is widely accepted as a key principle in building wealth. The historical meaning of multiple streams of income primarily includes any income an individual produces from a variety of unrelated sources. This proves to be a very powerful tool for people desiring to produce wealth.

Because of the Moose economy, things have changed. No longer does multiple streams of income provide the financial freedom it once did. As an employee, you are still able to use multiple streams of income and see the rewards and experience the benefits it produces, but because it is a stream of income, most often it is taxable as wages.

As a business owner, multiple streams of income is not as powerful as multiple streams of profit. The difference is, multiple streams of profits produce the added income without the added labor. For clarity, the meaning of multiple streams of profit refers only to sources of revenue generated by a business.

The key to this concept is to develop multiple sources of revenue without working more hours. For example, if you already work 40 hours per week at your regular job, for you to start another business (stream of income) working additional hours, you must increase your income to labor ratio, to increase the value of your time.

This is just two streams of income; add another stream (plus the hours) and you are in a category where few people can survive physically or mentally, because you cannot increase the equivalent number of hours for every stream of income you make. To develop these different revenue streams, you may consider some of the following:

**Additional products and services:** As a business owner you have the ability to add products and services and diversify your offerings. This works very well with consumable products.

**Rental property:** If you have the money to invest, rental income can become a very steady revenue stream.

**Royalties:** If you write a book, record an audio book, write an e-book, invent a product, etc., you can sell the rights and receive royalties for as long as distributors are selling your product.

**Build a business to sell:** Many business owners close the doors or dissolve their business simply because they get bored with it and want to move on to different interests. Build your business from the start in a way conducive to selling.

> As a business owner, multiple streams of income is not as powerful as multiple streams of profit.

**Internet:** Harness the power of the internet. There has recently been a mass movement of businesses toward the internet. The savvy home-based business owner will at the very least look into this as a viable option for his business. Some businesses, once established on a website, do not require the same hours of maintenance as conventional businesses, allowing the owner to pursue another web-based business if he so chooses.

**Build a residual income:** It is always good when you can do the work one time and get paid on a continuing monthly basis. Certain industries are geared toward producing residual incomes. For example, any business that sells cell phones secures the contract one time and is paid a monthly commission every time that bill is paid. Many other electronic services like satellite and cable television are designed similarly. Often nutritional products and a number of other products and services that are based on a monthly membership are available to be marketed and will provide a residual income.

# part 3

## the model
### *network marketing*

# chapter 7

## the history of
## network marketing

## chapter 7

# the history of
# network marketing

Network marketing, also referred to as direct sales, started virtually by accident in the early 1940's, just prior to America's involvement in World War II. There was a company in California called California Vitamins that was struggling to stay afloat with a limited number of sales people. They soon realized that their sales force consisted only of their original salesmen and a few family members of those salesmen. The family members joined the sales force simply because they liked the products and wanted to purchase them for themselves at the discounted rate. California Vitamins recognized the opportunity and decided to produce a compensation plan for those who would join the sales force and sell some of the products while finding others who would do the same.

They began marketing and distributing their vitamin products and offering payouts through multiple levels. This is where the Multi-Level Marketing (MLM) phrase began. So instead of hoping for one superstar salesman to come along they decided to use many salesmen, each selling a little at a time. This caught on with several different companies that still exist today. California Vitamins later changed their name to NutriLife. Two NutriLife distributors, Jay Van Andel and Rich DeVos, decided to leave NutriLife and start a company, and the Amway Corporation was born.

Amway is the company that fought the legal battles that ultimately resulted in the MLM industry being accepted as a legitimate business that moves products to the end consumer. Network marketing (which is the modern name for MLM) is actually taught as a viable business model by college professors who are graduates of Harvard Business School.

> Most network marketing companies adhere to marketing techniques that were developed in the 1950's.

The Amway Corporation enjoys great success. Over the years following its inception, this corporation grew to become one of the largest in a multi-billion dollar industry. During this time period, there were many companies that tried to duplicate Amway's business model. However, very few of those companies succeeded. This was due to a number of various problems, either with the company's business model or the product line itself.

Most network marketing companies adhere to marketing techniques that were developed in the 1950's. During this period in history, America was in a phase of great growth and prosperity. The war in Europe and Asia was over. Time and resources that were once designated to support the military's needs could now be directed toward everyday life.

Women were involved in the work force as never before, which meant there was more income for each household. This new rise in income increased the demand for goods and services, resulting in new products and services being developed daily. This produced a tremendous need to get these new products and services into the hands of consumers.

Families were very close and spent a great deal of time together at home. Friends and families visited on a regular basis, often without calling first. Gasoline was inexpensive, as were most things. People left their doors unlocked because they felt safe in the communities in which they lived.

People received their news from newspapers, radio, and television. These were the only mass media sources available for information, news, advertising, and announcements. The news agencies were trusted to deliver the truth. Advertising agencies utilized these three sources of media, but word of mouth was considered the ultimate way to advertise.

The handshake was as binding as a written contract. If a man gave you his word, it was as good as done. People interacted with one another to a much greater degree than they do today. When network marketing companies began to multiply, their methods of advertising included not only word of mouth but the three main media sources.

There is a proliferation of techniques passed down from one decade to the next. Some of the more ruthless practices have been rejected, but many of the early methods are still used in network marketing. Buying leads lists, newspaper ads, handing out thousands of business cards, cold calling, and a myriad of other methods have found their way into the arsenal of nearly every network marketing company. Some of these methods have proven to be a source of much frustration and fatigue for independent distributors.

Marketing techniques have changed dramatically in the past few years. Unfortunately, network marketing has not evolved along with the marketing strategies of the business world. The distributor who recognizes and acts upon these changes increases his probability of achieving financial success.

> Network marketing proves time and again to be one of the most credible, honorable, legal, and ethical ways to make a living.

Many pyramid schemes and scams, cunningly structured like network marketing, have flooded the market and consequently given the industry a bad name. Poor product offerings, bad business models, unsavory marketing practices, and a lack of integrity in the leadership of many of these companies simply added to the "stigma" that all network marketers use less-than-desirable business tactics. The overall opinion was that these companies are just schemes used by people who are trying to "get rich quick."

In reality, this could not be further from the truth. Network marketing proves time and again to be one of the most credible, honorable, legal, and ethical ways to make a living. Network marketing provides a way for many people to become a business owner with relatively low risk. The up-front investment for a network marketing business is usually very low. This low cost gives most people access to owning a business, regardless of their income bracket.

# chapter 8

## why network marketing?

**chapter 8**

# why network marketing?

W e understand that there are those who do not recognize certain people as an authority because they believe those people may be biased toward their personal interests. Many distributors quickly discover that it is difficult to recruit others and speak to prospects about network marketing because they have an apparent stake in someone joining their business. For those who would fall into that category, the following is some factual information from some unbiased authorities.

There are over 60 million people in more than 100 countries worldwide who are working in some type of network marketing business. The network marketing industry was recently reported to be responsible for more than $100 billion in annual sales. The newspaper, USA Today, ran an article in its May 14, 2009 issue about direct sales. They make some powerful statements. Almost everyone understands that our nation is currently experiencing very turbulent economic times. Charisse Jones, the author of the article "Want a recession-proof job? Think direct sales," says, "Direct-sales businesses that rely on home-based representatives to peddle their wares are seeing their sales forces rapidly expand as the nation's unemployment rate soars to nearly 9% and those who lost jobs and nest eggs look for new ways to make money."

People who are becoming home-based business owners are quickly realizing the benefits of business ownership. Not only are they experiencing the freedoms, tax breaks, and income possibilities, but when they are the owner of the business, they do not have to fear being laid off. This often becomes one of the major selling and recruiting points in the industry.

According to the Direct Selling Association, of the 60 million plus network marketers in the world, more than 15 million are working in the United States. Of the $100 billion in annual sales, nearly $31 billion was generated in the U.S. Even though the economy seems to continue spiraling downward, many network marketers have seen their businesses continue to grow.

> People who are becoming home-based business owners are quickly realizing the benefits of business ownership.

In a prominent national magazine, *Your Business At Home*, John Flemming says, "Each week, as many as 175,000 people in the United States, and as many as 300,000 people around the globe, decide to take advantage of the industry's exciting potential." (October 2008-Volume 3 - Issue 7 "The life you've been searching for" p. 9)This truly is a staggering number, yet this number represents less than one percent of the world's population, a number that is still minuscule in comparison to the number it will become. This is beginning to reveal a phenomenal shift in the workforce mentality from what it was just a few years ago.

Marketing strategies are in the midst of a great change. People are becoming numb to the marketing of the past. Large corporations are learning that television advertisements are proving less effective, and the marketing trend is beginning to swing back to one with a very personal touch. We inherently trust the people we know more than we trust some guy in a television advertisement. Our social nature dictates that we crave not only the attention of others, but also their advice and recommendations as well.

The marketing strategies of direct sales are changing. "Knocking on doors is history. Direct sales representatives now find new customers through such methods as referrals, gatherings and parties, spontaneous meetings on the street and the internet." (Charrise Jones, "Want a recession-proof job? Think direct sales" *USA Today*, May 14, 2009 sec. b p. 2)

Network marketing appeals to so many people because it is an income solution that can work with an already busy schedule. The two things most people feel they are lacking are time and money. This business model allows you to capitalize on your time and create an extra income at your convenience. Those who know enough people and are able to communicate well with others have been known to do very well. The self-motivated entrepreneurial types who have a large circle of influence sometimes pursue this kind of home-based business because the idea of being their own boss and making extra money is just too much to resist.

Network marketing provides great monetary benefits for the independent distributor. Because he now owns a business, the network marketer is able to take advantage of the business owner tax benefits. Many distributors realize a measure of personal freedom and control over their lives which is unavailable to employees. Their income is tied directly to their performance, which only drives them to work harder.

Some network marketing companies offer programs where there is no inventory to maintain or monthly sales quota to meet. Distributors earn commissions on their sales and on the sales of those whom they recruit into their organization. While many companies reward recruiting with bonuses, legitimate businesses do not compensate their representatives on recruitment alone.

Many compensation plans are very lucrative when two things occur. First, the company makes available great products and/or services, usually those already popular with consumers. Secondly, a distributor builds a sizable organization that produces a substantial volume of sales. These two factors often result in considerable commissions and bonuses. The low startup cost and low overhead involved in network marketing gives the average person the opportunity to achieve an above average income.

Network marketing is a social networking business. Many people go through life without a great deal of social interaction. We, as humans, are by nature social creatures. We need interaction in a social setting to grow, develop, and keep our sanity. As organizations grow, friendships are made and personal growth takes place that would not be likely in any other setting.

The growth of one's organization places him in a position to employ leverage. The larger his organization, the more he is able to leverage time, money, people and influence. Each kind of leverage is two-fold. First there is the leverage of his own time, money, person and influence. Then there is the leverage of other people's time, money, person, and influence. Being a network marketing business owner gives the distributor the power to capitalize on nearly every form of leverage.

> The low startup cost and low overhead involved in network marketing gives the average person the opportunity to achieve an above average income.

Some network marketing companies carry a diversified product line that is conducive to building multiple streams of income. When there is a wide range of products and services, the representatives are enabled to market each of those products and services, building an income from separate sources. If the company then chooses to change a service carrier or phase out an older product, the representative does not lose all his sales commissions and can easily transition to marketing the new product or service.

The products and services marketed by network marketing companies are often superior products in the marketplace. From nutritional products and home cutlery to energy and financial services, the superior quality gives distributors an advantage, and makes it easier for them to sell. In most cases representatives sell not only products and services, but also monthly memberships or recurring monthly supplies of the products and services. This is a wonderful benefit for the representatives, because as they make a sale, not only do they receive a commission for the sale, they receive another commission every time that customer pays for another month of that particular product or service.

Dan is a distributor for the network marketing company Acme Vitamins. He sells two vitamin packs to Bill and Nancy, (one for each of them). When he does, he sets them up for a monthly supply; as a result, he receives a commission for the sale of those two packs. After one month, Bill and Nancy see such a change in their metabolism and feel so much better that they decide to continue the daily regimen and purchase another month's supply. Dan now receives a commission payment every month Bill and Nancy purchase more vitamin packs. This is how network marketing can produce a residual income for you. You do the work only once, and your customers purchase the products and services monthly, which translates into a residual income.

There are some in the inner circles of network marketing companies who truly believe the best is yet to come. Whenever there is an economic upheaval, a massive transfer of wealth follows. We spoke earlier about the wealthy seeing things before they happen because they have a better vantage point from which to view current and future events. Historically, during a recession or depression, some people lose all, while others make their fortunes.

I believe there is a coming economic earthquake that will shake America at its core. Many businesses and businessmen will be brought low by this destructive wave through our economy. We have already begun to see the tremors preceding the massive quake. Some economists who believe that this Moose economy should be considered the warning track to prepare for what is ahead. Not only should individuals prepare, but corporations also should consider what marketing model will carry them through a desperately difficult economy.

Some of the largest corporations in the world have already partnered with direct sales companies to market their products. These corporations will experience a higher survival rate than those who hold to the traditional marketing venues. Not only that, but the individuals who market these products as network marketers also increase their chances of success in the turbulent times.

World famous business tycoon, Warren Buffet owns three direct sales companies and is quoted saying, "It is the best investment I ever made." Multi-billionaire Sir Richard Branson owns a network marketing company. Robert Kiyosaki and Donald Trump co-authored a book, and in it they recommend network marketing. Stephen Covey and Paul Zane Pilzner, both best selling authors, have acknowledged the incredible potential of direct sales. Pilzner believes, that in the next few years, many of the new millionaires in the U. S. will be made in the network marketing industry.

As time goes on and the turbulence continues, there will be an increasingly widening gap between successes and failures. Because of the marketing infrastructure provided by direct sales, companies and individuals who chose to utilize network marketing will ultimately position themselves for, not only their survival, but also for great success. We are on the verge of experiencing another great transfer of wealth. I also believe "the best is yet to come." If these famous and well informed businessmen are interested and involved in network marketing, why aren't you?

> Some of the largest corporations in the world have already partnered with direct sales companies to market their products.

A friend of mine once told me that there are only a few reasons why people do not see the potential and get started in network marketing: Arrogance, Ignorance, or Timing. Those who are arrogant feel that direct sales is below them. They believe they were created to do something so much greater than help others and become wealthy doing so.

The ignorant base their opinions on their misconceptions and misunderstandings, claiming that network marketing is a pyramid scheme or a scam. They think it is illegal because they have never taken the time to investigate beyond what others may have told them. Timing is the only legitimate reason someone may have for not immediately taking advantage of a direct sales opportunity. There are at times extenuating circumstances that are beyond the control of the individual. Life happens, and responsibilities require attention.

For an increasing number of people, timing is actually becoming more critical. The Moose economy has put savings and retirement funds in the tank, and people are becoming so disillusioned they can hardly tell which way is up. Now is the time to get started, take control and change your financial future.

Ben Stein once said, "It is inevitable that some defeat will enter even the most victorious life. The human spirit is never finished when it is defeated...it is finished when it surrenders." You must not become discouraged and surrender to the difficulties. Multitudes of employees feel boxed in at work, sitting in front of a machine all day. This often crushes their spirit and stifles their creativity. You must break free from the bondage of your "security" and chose to write your destiny. Your life is the paper, network marketing is the pen. All you have to do is pick up the pen and start writing.

# chapter 9

## elements of a good company

# chapter 9

# elements of
# a good company

### The Company

Many people do not know how to find the network marketing company that is right for them. If you are going to join yourself to a company it would be wise to learn as much about the company as you can. Your research should include certain aspects of the company such as their stability and longevity. A stable company is a financially solid, debt free organization.

You should look for a business that has been around for several years. This does not mean new companies cannot be stable and solid. Every company must have a beginning. However, the average lifespan of a new network marketing company is just over seven months. Less than five percent of new network marketing companies last longer than twenty four months. It is very important to look at the longevity of a company because no one wants to spend a year of their life building a business just to find out that the company is closing its doors due to instability or poor management. A good way to judge the stability of the company is to look at its ownership, management team, and financial standing.

There are two schools of thought when it comes to ownership of a company. A privately held business with no shareholders allows the

> A stable company is a financially solid, debt free organization.

management of the company to share more of the profits with its distributors, (those who are actually doing the work) but it has less scrutiny. A publicly owned company must be very transparent in its business practices. This makes it easier to find information about the company's ownership and financial status than a privately owned business. Unfortunately, they often focus most of their attention on the shareholders rather than the representatives.

You should also look for a company that has a good training program. If you are going to work with a company, there should at least be training material available for you to learn about your company, its products and/or services, and business tools or helps. You do not want to be involved in a company that pushes its distributors with hype and empty promises. Look for a company that markets a product or service that you can personally believe in. If you do not believe in what you are doing it is harder to succeed because it is obvious to prospective customers that you are putting on a show.

Many good network marketing companies offer products or services that are part of a very large and growing market. This plays a large role in the longevity of the company. For example, if you are a distributor for a company that sells and services Conestoga wagon wheels, at one point in history this would have been a large and rapidly growing market. But, we live in the twenty first century. The wheel still exists but the wagon wheel is an antiquity and novelty. This is not the market you want to be in to make a lot of money.

In order for a network marketing company to survive, it must offer a product that is consumable. If a product or service being offered is not consumable, there cannot be a recurring monthly income to the company by which to pay its representatives. The company would eventually fold because the payouts would overwork the income generated, regardless of the amount of the product or service. Many companies have offered good products, but these products were not consumable in nature.

Therefore, most of these companies either failed or had to restructure their product line offering.

Another thing to look for in a network marketing company is timing. By timing I mean, the timing of the product on the market. If your company markets a very unique brass door knob when the current styles of the day are bronze, your product is nearly useless. The company should always be researching, developing, and associating itself with products and services that reflect the trends of the times.

> Less than five percent of new network marketing companies last longer than twenty four months.

Another aspect of timing is when to join a company. Many people believe they have to get into a network marketing company on what they call the "ground floor" in order to be successful. For some companies this may be true; with the better network marketing companies, however, the time of entry into the company should not affect your level of success.

The management team should have integrity and should truly care about the success of the distributors and representatives that belong to the organization. Read the company's mission statement. This should be very clear about the intentions of the company and its leaders. Also, if it is available, find out what percentage of the revenues are paid out to the representatives. Another way to find out about the management of any company is to speak with the management team itself.

Sound business practices and integrity are vital to the foundation of any business. When companies close their doors due to a flaw in their business practices, it is devastating to the representatives. They worked hard to build their organizations and ultimately lose everything they worked for because of faulty practices. When looking for the network marketing company that is right for you, you should look for the following characteristics:

1.  Proven to stand the test of time.

2.  Financially solid. No/low debt service.

3. Strong corporate support structure.

4. Leadership with integrity and experience.

5. Good ratings from independent (watch-dog) organizations such as Better Business Bureau, Dunn & Bradstreet, etc.

6. Transparency about mission and vision.

7. Strong compensation plan that includes both a residual and bonus structure which puts representatives first. (This encourages the representatives to work hard because they can know what to expect for their achievements.)

8. Multi-product diversity. (A variety of products and/or services that a great majority of the population is already using.)

9. Provides products and services that lend themselves to a recurring nature. (Because people are conditioned to unconsciously pay their monthly bills, it is more appealing when they do not have to think about repurchasing or replenishing their supply or services. They are marketed one time and the sale occurs month after month. This leads to a true residual income.)

10. Simplified responsibilities of the representatives. (The representatives are not required to produce, inventory, deliver, or collect for the products and services they market. The task of the representatives should be purely marketing, not manufacturing, warehousing, financing, delivering or collections.)

There are several companies that pass this close scrutiny with flying colors. While some companies are better than others, it is not the purpose of this book to compare the opportunities that exist in the network marketing industry. Instead, this book is designed to give relevant and pertinent information to those individuals who are interested in gaining knowledge about this industry or perhaps have been struggling with getting a business off the ground. This book is written to give the person who is starting a network marketing business an educated edge toward success.

## Compensation Plan

Any great network marketing company is set apart by a compensation plan that includes not only a long-term residual income, but also an up-front bonus system that allows its representatives to enjoy fruits of their labors as quickly as possible. Most compensation plans pay to at least four levels deep. The better the compensation plan, the more levels on which the company will pay. There are some companies that actually pay to unlimited levels and still have the up-front bonus system in place.

> Sound business practices and integrity are vital to the foundation of any business.

If you are already a representative in network marketing, look at the pay structure available to you and ask if the pay plan has expanded over time, and if it will continue to expand into the future. If it is truly expanding, the payouts to the representatives will continue to get better. If the company is cutting back on its pay plan, beware. When a company is struggling financially, representative compensation is one of the first things to go.

## Products and Services

The products and services of great network marketing companies have a few qualities in common. First, they carry products that are used on a weekly, if not daily basis. They are products and services used on a very large scale. At a minimum the products or services should be available regionally, the best case being nation wide or even internationally. This creates the largest possible pool of prospective clients and potential new distributors.

Whatever the product or service, it does not have to be manufactured, produced or provided by the network marketing company itself. There are many great name brand products that are marketed by network marketing businesses that have no production ties to one another.

Some companies carry a "buffet" of sorts in their product and service line. This makes them great because, inevitably, trends will dictate change. When a company is not tied to one specific product, and it loses one for any reason, it can simply pick up a new product that is "hot" on the market and continue to thrive.

## What to Avoid

When searching for the best network marketing opportunity, you will want to avoid several things. Stay away from a company that does not have a viable product or service. These businesses are often schemes, which are illegal. A network marketing company that partners with major corporations has already been investigated by these corporation's highly paid attorneys. There is little chance these corporations are going to be connected in any way to some "fly-by-night" operation that is here today and gone tomorrow.

> One of the most important aspects of any network marketing company is the representatives.

Once you have joined the company of your choice, move forward in every avenue possible. Any distributor should adhere closely to the policies set forth by their company. These policies are established to protect and to serve not only the company but also the representatives. A multitude of legal issues can be avoided if the distributors will simply stay within the bounds set forth by their company.

One of the more problematic issues to avoid is "projecting" incomes. Projecting an income is when a representative reveals or displays his income to a potential representative to "show him" what he could be making some day. Though it is possible for the new representative to make the same amount or more, the law prohibits leading him to sign up under this pretense. The new representative may never achieve the same pay level and may therefore, feel he was tricked into the business.

Some people have made false claims about their company's products. This often happens when a company's product line is built around the nutrition industry. For example, an uneducated representative claims that his product will cure cancer or heal the body of a certain disease.

The Food and Drug Administration enforces laws which forbid any food or drink to claim healing properties for a disease or to cure an ailment, unless it is classified as a pharmaceutical drug. Since legal drugs can only be purchased over the counter, network marketing companies are not allowed to sell or distribute them. Thus, any nutritional products sold and distributed must not be represented as a cure or healing agent.

While there are various pitfalls to avoid in network marketing, there is one problem area that affects people the most. This pitfall is when people join the first direct sales business that is presented to them. For one reason or another, they do not realize there are other possibilities available and that if they simply checked them out they would find the one that is the most comfortable fit for them. This is not to say that the first business opportunity is not the best. You should simply do your homework and prevent yourself from being one of those who fail or quit because it "just didn't work out."

There are many characteristics that make up a strong network marketing company. Only a few of them have been listed in this chapter. One of the most important aspects of any network marketing company is the representatives. People follow other people, and the real strength of any company lies in the character and integrity of the people who are associated with it. If the company business model, pay structure, integrity, or any other major characteristic is flawed, it will not be long before you begin to see people "jumping ship."

# part 4

## the marketer
### *the core of the network marketing business*

# chapter 10

## essential qualities of network marketing professionals

## chapter 10

# essential qualities of network marketing professionals

Have you ever heard someone say, "This would be a good place to work if it weren't for the people?" I know we laugh at this, but the truth is that people do make or break a company and/or its reputation. The difference in traditional and network marketing companies is that while traditional companies can choose who works for them, network marketing companies do not have this luxury.

As a whole, the type of person who joins a network marketing company is typically a self-starter who has a high level of internal motivation and can handle, or even prefers, working alone. This is not to say he is anti-social. He simply has the courage to be different from the average employee. Because network marketing is not typically someone's first choice for a career right out of college, time and circumstances usually create the realization that network marketing is a good fit for financial "Plan B."

I have enjoyed the outdoor activity of gold prospecting for many years. One of the things you learn quickly is to look for black sand when searching for a good place to prospect. Black sand is simply grains of iron the same size as sand particles. The reason you look for black sand is that, like gold, it is heavier than regular dirt and sand particles. This similarity allows a prospector to deduce the approximate travel pattern gold may be moving in a creek or river bed.

There are a couple types of common iron sand: hematite and magnetite. Using this as an analogy for human behavior and personality, we could say there are hematite people and magnetite people. When you refer to someone with a hematite personality, it is a good thing. A hematite person may have strong values and be the backbone of the company.

A magnetite person, on the other hand, not only has a strong personality, but also attracts others to him. Magnetite is the most magnetic of all the natural minerals. It is an iron ore, so it too is very strong. Magnetite people are leaders with strong values who know how to help others achieve more.

> The truth is that people do make or break a company and/or its reputation.

The corporate world is rampant with the "dog eat dog" mentality. Competition is fierce and very unforgiving. Though it is a difficult arena, magnetite people do very well in this environment. Network marketing is designed in such a way that when you join, the more you help others, the better you will do.

This atmosphere is fertile soil for magnetite people because helping others is what network marketing is all about. Because of the environment found in network marketing, magnetic people are drawn to become distributors. These magnetic distributors then draw other strong personalities into the business, making an even greater setting in which to work.

There are many kind, helpful, competent, and (needless to say) wealthy representatives in network marketing. One main reason for this is because many of those in network marketing were professionals before they joined their business of choice. They carried with them a level of professionalism and courtesy when they started their business.

This means that, before they joined, they already had a desire to help others, a vision for their future. They were willing to work hard and unwilling to quit. They developed their leadership skills and understood that it takes a team effort. They had good morals and ethics, strong character and a good reputation.

If you are going to become a network marketer of this caliber, you must, like them, desire to help yourself, your children and grandchildren. You must commit to working at it and understand that success does not come easily. As a distributor, you must hold the standard high. You must be honest, have integrity, and practice good morals. Since starting your business depends solely on your actions, you must build a good reputation by having character.

Dress to portray a professional image. Project this image with a neat and clean appearance, and conduct yourself in a professional manner. You will have to be bigger than any problems. Professional people do not complain to others in their business. They learn to help others and understand that rejection is nothing more than wounded self love.

For some, becoming the professional will require learning marketing skills. These marketing skills will not only grow their business, but also will help them in their customer acquisitions. Others will have to concentrate on personal development. As a person learns and grows, he is more apt to become a leader and begin teaching others what he learned.

> There are many kind, helpful, competent, and (needless to say) wealthy representatives in network marketing.

Leadership is a necessity because any time a group takes action, decisions must be made and a direction must be chosen. If there is no leader to make the decision, or at least to officiate the debate, there will be nothing but mass confusion. A leader never imposes his vision on others. He may share with them his vision to help them catch a vision for themselves.

The network marketer is also very patient with others. People are the heart and soul of network marketing. Because everyone is different, network marketers recognize these differences as strengths and not as weaknesses. When you build on the strengths of others, it results in a much stronger organization.

One of the most outstanding characteristics I have seen in network marketers is the willingness to help others. If this is not prevalent in your organization, there could be more troublesome problems just below the surface. Helping others is a quality that duplicates itself naturally. When people receive help and respond by helping others, this helping mentality grows exponentially in just a short period of time.

> Helping others is a quality that duplicates itself naturally.

Regardless of the company, products, or pay plan, one thing will always remain in the ranks of most organizations: the depth of unity and harmony in most groups, and the true professionalism that is characteristic of most people who call themselves network marketers.

# chapter 11

## personal development

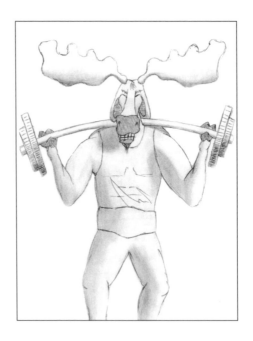

**chapter 11**

# personal development

**P**ersonal development is essential to building good relationships that affect the outcome of your business. Personal development occurs when you decide to add positively to your knowledge, looks, personality, character, or behavior.

You are responsible for your personal development. Choosing to better yourself increases your chances of success and positions you to help others. One of the most important decisions you make in personal development is the people with whom you choose to associate. These people become the standard by which you are measured because they influence your behavior. Your associations also affect your influence on others.

You are influenced either positively or negatively by the people with whom you associate. The people you allow into your circle of influence not only reflect, but affect your outlook on life, which determines the type of people you attract. Since negative people are always negative, you must strive to attract only those who are positive. Negative people influence your decisions, and make it difficult to lead your organization. A positive outlook in life and business will help you seize new opportunities, because "Opportunities never go away; they just move from one person to the next."

## *Business Practices*

People are not the only aspect of personal development that affect your success. Regardless of the opportunities available, there are principles which should guide you in your business. The following three areas of personal development are crucial to success:

1. Ethical Business Practices

2. Marketing Techniques

3. Company Policies and Procedures

The practice of ethics is a fading quality in the "dog-eat-dog" world of business. Recent news revealed stories of unethical business practices resulting in government intervention. The network marketing industry has its fair share of unethical people, resulting in some network marketing companies acquiring a bad reputation. Nothing should deter you from ethical business practices.

> "Opportunities never go away; they just move from one person to the next."

Unethical business practices cause skepticism outside the network marketing industry. These practices give the industry a "black eye" and make it very difficult for those running a legitimate business to present their products or services as such. Therefore, misleading statements, false claims, and pushy sales tactics hurt everyone in the long run and should be avoided.

Some people have completely severed ties from traditional marketing methods. This decision will prove to be a detriment to their business. Traditional marketing methods still have their place in the arsenal of the network marketer; however, many of the traditional uses for these methods must be re-thought. Network marketing companies should expand their policies to embrace these new electronic methods of marketing.

Every distributor should understand and adhere to his company's policies and procedures. Policies and procedures are established to keep representatives from stepping over boundaries and laws developed for the protection of the consumer. Navigating outside these rules may subject you to possible legal action. As long as you follow the rules and regulations of the company, you are less likely to run into trouble. It is not necessary for you to commit the policies and procedures to memory, but understanding them will enable you to guide your downline (representatives you recruit into your organization) into safe business practices.

You should acquire certain disciplines that set you apart from ordinary network marketing distributors. You can establish yourself as a leader when you are willing to go the extra mile to gain insights that help you make good decisions, lead by example, motivate, and protect the investment you make in other people. A disciplined leader will help his business partners be successful by conducting meetings, training new representatives, and hosting teleconferences. Many times a leader will need to do things that are not pleasant or convenient, but necessary to help their organization grow and run successfully.

> Traditional marketing methods still have their place in the arsenal of the network marketer.

Local weekly meetings are critical to the growth of any network marketing business. Because network marketing is a relationship business rather than a traditional brick and mortar business, conducting meetings at a place like the local Marriott gives your business an upscale presence at least once a week. Conducting meetings outside your local area can be very costly and time consuming. This practice should be reserved for later in your business when your income can better support such activities.

Training is an essential part of the growth of your organization. Some training can be performed over the phone. However, leading by example requires a leader to be "in the trenches" so new representatives can learn by duplication. The ability to train others is essential to the leadership role.

Good disciplines should include good time management, good work habits, taking responsibility for your actions, and knowing when to say no. Time management is one of the most elusive disciplines. It is easy to allow nonessential activities into your daily routine, robbing you of precious time.

Time management and personal development are intertwined. As a home-based business owner, you have much more freedom, and, therefore, much more opportunity for distraction. Personal development is a vital part of the business because it provides you with skills to slay the raging moose. However, too much personal development can stifle productivity. There must be a balance between personal development and personal time.

### Work Habits

Good work habits must be learned and will help eliminate lost time. They also help dispel fear and anxiety of the unknown. There is security in routine, even in uncertainty. Good habits can be passed from one person to the next, resulting in a stronger organization.

Good work habits include:

1. Setting aside time each week to work your business.

2. Following up with contacts.

3. Reading and learning about your company and the industry.

4. Supporting the downline.

5. Sharing information with others.

The goal of personal development is to become a person who can better interact with others. Personal development involves more than just learning. It requires decisive action to produce constant growth as a citizen, family member, and business owner.

Some people have tried network marketing and failed. But, as Paul Orberson, founder and president of Fortune Hi Tech Marketing says, "You try peas and carrots; you don't try network marketing; you just get in and do it." There are a number of reasons that contribute to the failure of any venture. Some people, like the field guide, know where to look and when to seize the right opportunity. Others like the dentist get lucky and finally kill the moose. And yet the majority run out of ammunition before obtaining the prize.

Network marketing is not an easy business, but it is simple. Representatives who wish to be successful in network marketing must spend time gaining knowledge about the industry. Researching on the internet, participating in seminars, and building a good library of books and resources about network marketing will go a long way toward personal growth and development. The distributor who continually reads books, newspaper and magazine articles may some day be written about in those same publications. A good knowledge of network marketing does not guarantee success, but successful representatives know a great deal about the industry.

# chapter 12

## your values

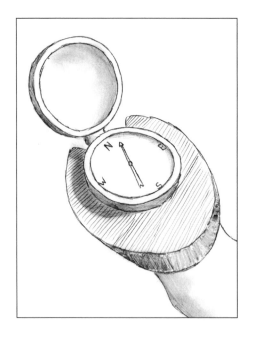

# chapter 12

# your values

A sense of good moral values and ethical business practices will serve as an internal compass for you. Just as the needle of a compass always points north, good moral values and high standards of ethics will always point to the high road in business practices. Your moral compass will be an invaluable tool that you must protect and guard as part of your survival gear in a Moose economy.

Morals are the principles of right and wrong which govern our behavior. Our moral values are what cause us to feel good and have a sense of internal reward when we do the right thing. Likewise, these values produce feelings of guilt when we act against them.

We are all born with an inherent sense of morals, and we develop morals through knowledge. For example, a child knows not to reach for a forbidden object, but, when he does and is caught and disciplined, he learns to discern right from wrong. This correction and discipline establishes a moral value as a benchmark of expected behavior.

Religion is also responsible for providing moral values. For centuries, religious establishments have set standards according to their beliefs. These standards flow into the immediate society and become adopted by the people. Often these standards come in the form of lists of "do's" and "don'ts." For some, the standard is based on maintaining a relationship with a holy God.

Morals are applied on the personal level and practiced in private as well as in public. When moral standards spill over into social situations and business practices, they can be referred to as ethics. Ethics are the standards of right and wrong as determined by society. Most of the time, morals and ethics work hand in hand and are virtually indistinguishable, but there are cases where ethics supersede morals. Because a business or government requires certain actions to be performed, personal morals may have to be set aside as that action is taken.

> Morals are the principles of right and wrong which govern our behavior.

For example, a social worker may not agree that a child should be removed from a home where the court deemed necessary, but it is the duty of that social worker to carry out the command of the court. Ethics demand that the personal beliefs and morals of the worker be laid aside for the good of the child and to uphold the justice system. While this is not the norm, it does happen.

Most of the time, network marketers deal with ethics in two main areas, the first is the issue of money. For whatever reason, people who are in business for themselves struggle with properly handling money when they lack ethical standards. Embezzlement and tax evasion are two offenses often cited when the issue of money and ethics are found in the same sentence.

The second issue is the matter of recruiting. In the majority of network marketing businesses, one of the largest tasks is finding new representatives. A network marketer who is not guided by ethical standards will often skew or stretch the truth in order to appeal to prospective representatives.

Although something may be unethical, it is not necessarily illegal. At the same time, though a certain action may be legal, it is not always the right thing to do. Every situation is different, but when someone is guided by good ethics and morals his actions will reflect those values.

Moral actions are branded with honesty and integrity. Mary Kay Ash, the founder of Mary Kay Cosmetics said, "Honesty is the cornerstone of all success, without which confidence and ability to perform shall cease to exist." At times you will be faced with a decision to choose between honesty and dishonesty. It is at that time when your integrity will help you make the right decision.

For example, virtually everyone has been met with a situation where it was perceived that personal gain could be made by looking the other way or stretching the truth. Often this comes in the form of an easy dollar or even a promotion in the workplace. Should that person choose to pursue the personal gain, though he may consider himself to be a good person, in the end he will begin to reflect on his dishonesty. Ultimately, he will have to answer the question: was the decision to do wrong worth the guilt it produced?

> If honesty is the principle, integrity is the backbone.

Honesty and integrity work hand in hand. If honesty is the principle, integrity is the backbone. Without integrity, an honest person may shy away from the truth in a high pressure situation. Without honesty, there is no integrity in a person's character.

Honesty and integrity are developed internally and revealed externally. You can tell someone you have integrity and that you are honest, but until you perform according to your word, there is no substance to your claim. People will not believe what you say until they see what you do.

A person of integrity lives a life of openness and truth and is known for being genuine. He has nothing to hide because his actions are above reproach. His judgments are sound because he makes his decisions on strong values. You will become known as a person of honesty and integrity when you make it a policy to tell the truth and hold uncompromisingly to your values.

You may be asking yourself why you need to practice honesty and integrity. Who cares about good moral values and ethics these days? It is simple. As a network marketing business owner, you will be a leader. Influencing others is at the heart of leadership. To influence others you must have credibility with them. To establish credibility, you must first gain their trust. People inherently trust a genuinely honest person. Good morals and ethics displayed by honesty and integrity produce that trust.

Being honest with others begins with being honest with yourself. It is human nature to view others in the same light in which you view yourself. A dishonest person always feels others are dishonest with him. The danger with being dishonest is not only that others would not trust you, but that you could not trust them. Therefore, your level of trust in others may be a gauge of your honesty and integrity.

> Influencing others is at the heart of leadership.

Honesty and integrity are but two qualities of character. A person's character can be defined as the sum of his behavioral traits that govern how he will react to various situations. Someone who has character could be described as also having courage, compassion, honor, and good ethics.

Character is a learned behavior. There are traits which can be nurtured to become a part of the person who fosters them. These traits often give a person identity because they govern his reaction in various situations. A person's character dictates whether he will complete a task or quit half way through and whether or not he will be honest with others and obey the rules and laws of the land. Helen Keller said, "Character cannot be developed in ease and quiet. Only through experience of trial and suffering can the soul be strengthened, ambition inspired, and success achieved."

The Josephson Institute of Ethics defines six pillars of character. These pillars are the foundation on which someone's character is built.

1. Trustworthiness: Being a person worthy of trust as a result of honesty, integrity and loyalty.

2. Respect: Giving others the respect they deserve as well as respecting yourself. Having dignity and practicing courtesy.

3. Responsibility: Performing your duty, and being accountable for your actions. Always doing your best.

4.  Fairness: Being open minded, impartial and just. Playing by the rules and not taking advantage of others.

5.  Caring: Practicing kindness and compassion for others. Safeguarding the well being of others is placed above the desire to win.

6.  Citizenship: Obeying and upholding the law. Participating in civic duties. Being a good neighbor.

Good character builds a good reputation. Though character and reputation are not the same, they are directly linked together. Your character is who you are when no one else is around, while your reputation is how others perceive you. Your character strongly influences your reputation while your reputation has little or no bearing on your character. Abraham Lincoln said, "Character is like a tree and reputation like its shadow. The shadow is what we think of it; the tree is the real thing."

A good name is one of the most valuable assets that a person or business can possess. It is because of a good name that people trust that person or business. Nike, Mercedes Benz, Caterpillar, and Motorola have built a reputation by making good products and therefore have a good name. Customers trust them for quality engineering and service.

A reputation takes years to build and only seconds to destroy. You must protect your reputation from being blemished. In order to survive in the Moose economy, your character must be one of honesty and integrity.

# chapter 13

## your appearance

# chapter 13

# your appearance

It is important to dress properly for a hunting trip. The hunter dressed in swim trunks and cowboy boots not only looks ridiculous but stands a strong chance of immediate failure. Anyone who has endured the torment of hiking through the wilderness in the heat of summer, battling through the brambles, swinging at the gnats and mosquitoes and navigating the uneven terrain, can appreciate the importance of being properly dressed.

If the hunter were to actually dress this way we would consider him foolish. If he wanted to succeed, he would begin by choosing the right clothing. Yet, many business people fail to dress in a way that promotes their success.

It is important that you know how to dress appropriately. Overdressing makes for awkwardness, while under dressing can send a message of indifference. You would not go to a formal awards ceremony dressed in cut-offs and flip flops, nor would you attend an informal garden party in a three piece suit.

Today, dress codes and standards are more ambiguous than ever. Because our society is moving away from the conservative values of the past, standards of appearance and conduct are now more vague and lacking in distinction. Many people fail to realize that how they dress sets them apart and speaks volumes about their character. The way you dress subconsciously reflects the way you feel. This is why so many styles and descriptions of clothing are tied directly to emotions. (Frumpy, classy, hot, cool, comfortable, cheery. etc.)

People judge a book by its cover; likewise, they will judge you by how you dress. Being dressed properly will help you project a successful image. Though the phrase "dress for success," may be a cliché, the idea is still under-exploited and ignored when it could be helpful to many network marketers. Your clothing affects not only how you are perceived, but also how well you are received. Your appearance can influence others in either a positive or negative way. The following are some simple rules to consider when choosing what to wear.

> Many business people fail to dress in a way that promotes their success.

1. Consider the circumstances. Make sure you are aware of the conditions and expectations of your role in the occasion.

2. Conservative styles are always safe. This is not because everyone has conservative taste, but because wearing conservative clothing is less offensive in most situations.

3. Dress to emphasize professionalism and aptitude, not to attract attention to your taste in clothing.

4. Your clothing should add to your appearance and compliment your features rather than detract from them.

5. Dress comfortably. If you appear to be uncomfortable, chances are your audience will be too.

6. Do not spell "casual" s-l-o-p-p-y. When your clothes look sloppy you risk being perceived as a sloppy person.

Another phrase that is over-used and under-valued is "you never get a second chance to make a first impression." We have already established that people judge a book by its cover and that your attire is the cover to your book. When speaking of first impressions, it is important to dress in a way that creates a desirable opinion.

First impressions are usually the first building block of any business relationship. We have previously established that the emphasis of network marketing should be on marketing. Before you can market your products, you must first market yourself. Once you sell yourself, selling your products is usually much easier.

Judging a book by the cover is almost instantaneous, an opinion of a website only takes a few seconds, and at a glance, you are sized up by how you dress. On average, people take less than a minute to form an opinion about another person. Right or wrong, it only takes a few seconds for us to evaluate or judge a person's credibility and potential performance.

> Your clothing affects not only how you are perceived, but also how well you are received.

Knowing this, you should do everything you can to project a positive image. When creating the image you want others to see, attention to detail is absolutely critical. There are three areas of your image that will be scrutinized and judged when you are introduced to someone. First, others look at your clothing; secondly, they notice your hygiene; and thirdly, they observe your conduct.

### Clothing:

1. You do not need the wardrobe of a superstar, just the basics will do.

2. If you must purchase additional clothing to dress appropriately, start with just a couple of outfits to stay within your budget.

3. Make sure your clothes fit properly. Clothing that is too loose or too tight may send the wrong message.

4. Wear your best. The clothes you wear should be pressed, free of blemishes, holes and stains, and in good condition.

5. Put your best foot forward. If you wear shoes that can be polished, polish them. Otherwise make sure your shoes are at least clean.

6. Keep the jewelry to a minimum. You are trying to attract attention to yourself not your bling.
(Sorry, Mr. T!)

### Hygiene:

1. Hands and face: Be neat and clean in appearance. Ladies: use minimal makeup. Men: trim the beard and shave the face. Wash hands, and use lotion if necessary.

2. Smile: Brush your teeth and make sure you have fresh breath. Be discreet with chewing gum and mints.

3. Hair: Should be kempt. Comb it, brush it, and use gel or hairspray. Avoid unnatural colors and mohawks.

4. Fingernails: Men: clean the grime out from under your fingernails and trim them. Ladies: fingernails should be clean, trimmed and painted.

5. Body Odor: Unfortunately, everyone deals with this. Shower regularly and use deodorant.

6. Cologne/Perfume: Body odors are not the only smells that can be offensive. Keep colognes and perfumes to a minimum. You might think it smells good, but not everyone shares your opinion.

## Conduct:

1.  Act the part: You should be the expert and authority in your business.

2.  Posture: Not only should you sit up straight, but you should teach yourself to stand with your shoulders back and head high. This helps you promote confidence in yourself and look the part of the business owner.

3.  Body Language: Watch your attitude - confident, not cocky. Your body language speaks volumes without you saying a word.

4.  Handshake: Shake other people's hands with purpose and energy. This does not mean to jerk their arm out of socket, but do not give them a dead fish to shake either.

5.  Eye Contact: Look others in the eye. Only those who are ashamed, defeated, or guilty do not look someone in the eye when they shake hands.

6.  Listening Skills: A true leader realizes the importance of and practices good listening skills. Nothing will endear your audience to you more than the act of sincerely listening to them.

There are always exceptions to the rules. For instance, it is better to have a piece of gum or a mint rather than bad breath. Be sure to dress, look and act your best and you will be off to a good start.

The goal is to strive for a professional image. You want people to see you as qualified as possible. Since perception is reality, your image is anything people see about you and your business. This is not limited to your clothing, hygiene or conduct. It can also include your website, business cards, advertisements, company logo and graphics, vehicle (especially if it has any business related print on it), and promotional items.

# chapter 14

## first aid

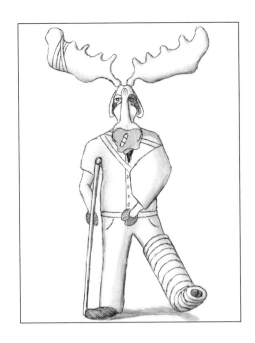

# chapter 14

# first aid

O ne of the most important items in your business will be your first aid kit. Your emotional and financial first aid kit should be equipped with measures to help you prevent and recover from the unexpected. This does not mean that you carry a band-aid around in your pocket, but that you will prepare yourself with a number of things to help you recover from events that might hurt you.

First aid is simply the provision of preliminary care administered to someone with an injury or illness. In day-to-day life, we administer first aid for a number of reasons, ranging from superficial injuries to life threatening emergencies. First aid is not limited to physical injuries. The concept of first aid can also be applied to network marketing.

People often fail to understand the relevance of first aid to network marketing. The application of first aid may save your business while in the Moose economy. The purpose of first aid is two fold: to preserve life and to promote recovery. The most important principle is knowing what to do and how to respond in each situation.

Emotional trauma from rejection and failure is common in network marketing. Representatives who try to promote their business only to be turned away and ridiculed for their efforts can suffer emotionally and, consequently, may resort to negativity and disparagement. Criticism and skepticism are two hurdles that network marketers must overcome. Someone who is critical of others often lacks knowledge and understanding. Criticism is often a result of a perceived threat or competition. Skepticism is the attitude of doubt rooted in disbelief. While skepticism may provide a sense of security, it is not wise to be closed-minded.

Some skeptics will approach you with valid questions and bring factual information to the discussion. You should listen to them with the respect they deserve by giving them your undivided attention and answering their questions sincerely and truthfully. You will find that closed-minded skeptics are irrational, rejecting any logical argument. Do not worry yourself with them because there is no reasoning that will convince them. Sadly, some network marketers perceive these hurdles as walls they cannot overcome.

> The application of first aid may save your business while in the Moose economy.

Emotional damage can come from countless sources. People are wounded by their friends, their enemies, and even their own actions. Many network marketers harm their business by making poor decisions. Others are hurt and offended when things do not go their way. These people pout and have a "pity party" when they do not get what they want or when someone betters them at their game.

Economic stress, caused by changes in the economy, can affect every aspect of personal finances and play a large role in the daily life of the individual. However, every American has the right to determine his future by controlling his individual financial decisions. A distinction should be drawn between finances and economics. Although both affect everyone, only personal finances can be controlled by the individual.

There are times when circumstances will require you to administer financial first aid. Inflation, deflation, gas prices, a housing bust, and a recession can affect the working class. Family and health issues can be complicated by the financial strain they produce. Financial stress often comes in the form of unexpected loss or expenses, which have become commonplace in this Moose economy.

# first aid

Because our founding fathers had the wisdom to root our economy in capitalism, we enjoy the liberty of owning our time. We are not enslaved to a communist or socialist economic system, forcing us to work for predetermined wages. Americans are among the few people on earth who are free to name their price and choose to accept a job or move on to the next, in search for better pay.

As a participant in the business world, you must accept the responsibility of administering first aid, whether it is to yourself or others. In a survival situation, refusing to help someone in need of medical attention would be very selfish. As a good citizen you would instinctively take measures to stop the bleeding and help the injured deal with the pain.

> Through network marketing, you have the opportunity to change your future by owning a business.

This also applies to financial and economic trauma. You must first stop the bleeding (loss of income) and deal with the pain (debt); only then can you begin to recover. Network marketing provides the system that enables the average person to administer financial first aid to himself, as well as to those in need around him.

The need for financial and economic first aid can be minimized by the preventative measures you have in place. Taking care of a problem before it happens saves not only time and money, but also a lot of heartache later on. Several preventative measures that can be instituted are having an emergency fund, developing multiple streams of income, and having a system in place that continues to work even when you cannot.

Through network marketing, you have the opportunity to change your future by owning a business. The relatively low startup cost and overhead allows you to grow your business and earn an income without going bankrupt. Network marketing enables you to use leverage and often produces multiple streams of income, giving you the power to change your financial position.

Most importantly, be watchful for those in need. First aid is more than a necessity; it is the responsibility of every good citizen. I recently visited a wealthy friend of mine. When I arrived, he was in his garden.

The weeds had nearly taken over and he was working frantically to get rid of them. I jumped right in and started helping him and before too long we had the garden back in shape and his vegetables had a fighting chance for survival. I left that day not thinking much about it–I enjoy gardening, so it was actually fun for me.

At the time of my visit, I did not know he had fallen on hard times. I spoke with him again two weeks later. He told me that the day I came to visit he was at one of the lowest points he had ever been in his life. My actions had encouraged him so much he was not able to put it into words.

He was struggling not only with the garden, but also in keeping up with his house, his bills, and many other things. Just the simple act of being there for my friend encouraged him to keep going. If you will only be watchful and willing to help others, your business will grow and thrive. Keep your first aid kit handy; others will thank you for it.

# part 5

## mooseology
### *the survival guide*

# chapter 15

## survival basics

*"plan your trip" (for success)*

# survival basics

### *"plan your trip" (for success)*

This survival guide is designed to educate and to equip you for greater success in your network marketing business. Success is a relative term. To some, success means total financial freedom; to others, it is fame and fortune, yet there are those who feel successful with a little extra income with which to go to the movies or out to eat every other weekend. You must decide in the planning stage what success means to you.

Like the dentist, you have the opportunity to prepare for your "moose" hunt. This could be one of the most thrilling adventures ever experienced in your lifetime. With a Moose economy, the outcome may be unpredictable, but your actions will greatly influence the result. With any trip, you must begin in the planning stage by identifying the reason for going, developing an itinerary for your travel, and executing your plan. So, plan your trip for success!

Anyone choosing network marketing as an income solution should understand what the business is all about. The uneducated representative touts his business, products and services as virtually "selling themselves." Network marketing is not about products and services; it is about marketing products and services. Mooseology is designed to help educate distributors in the network marketing industry.

Your job as a network marketer is to build an organization of people who facilitate the transfer of goods and services from producer to consumer. Marketing is the creation of product appeal targeting specific consumers. Unfortunately, the only concept many network marketers have learned is that if enough people see the products and services, accompanied with a compensation plan, their business will flourish. This idea has proven effective, but without taking advantage of available marketing tools, the average person's "circle of influence" is too small to accommodate the learning curve needed to effectively grow their business. Lack of education in marketing led to widespread failures in the industry.

> Your job as a network marketer is to build an organization of people who facilitate the transfer of goods and services from producer to consumer.

## Ready-Why Go Anyway?

Regardless of your definition of success, you must have a reason to put forth an effort to achieve success. Anyone satisfied with the status quo will only achieve ordinary results. If you want something different out of life, you must be willing to do something different. If you want more than the average person has, you must do more than the average person does.

One way to accomplish this is to become a business owner. In network marketing, as in any business, you must determine why you want to work that particular business. This "why" is your main reason for devoting your time, talents, resources, and energy to what you are doing.

Establishing a why is very important because of what it does for you. Your why gives you direction and keeps you on course when times get tough. Though your why does not guarantee your success, it is the source of your resolve and determination. It should inspire you and remind you of your purpose and vision. It is this resolution that finds the ways to succeed when the odds are seemingly stacked against you. Here is a list of ideas to guide you to establishing your why.

1.  Recognize your dreams and establish your goals. Ask yourself, if money and time were no object, what would you contribute to the world, what would you want to accomplish in your life, or what activities would you plan with your family?

2.  Identify why you are pursuing your business. Make a list of the things you plan to do when you reach different levels of success.

3.  Make this list visible. For some it works best to print the list out. For others they must create a collage of photos and pictures that represent their list. Regardless, find the way that works best for you and post it where you will see it every day.

Your why is the first key to survival in network marketing. Make your picture of success very specific and visual. If it is unclear and non-specific, your results will often reflect the same. I have heard a number of whys from many different representatives. Some of them include paying for my children's education, letting my spouse stay home, early retirement, paying off the house early, getting or staying out of debt, spending more time with my children/grandchildren, travelling the world, and so on. Your why must be bigger in your mind than any challenges that will come your way.

You should set goals and identify the tasks that will help you reach those goals. Be very specific; for example, narrow your aspirations from "some day I want to make lots of money" to "within one year, I want to increase my income by twenty percent." When your goals are specific, you are able to identify the steps necessary to achieve them. Now that you know you want to increase your income by twenty percent you can establish a list of tasks that will lead to that increase. Since you know that you want to do it within the coming year, you can set a time-line for completing each task.

Some goals will be universal to all network marketers regardless of the company. Your why influences your goals, and answering the following questions may help you identify them.

1.  How much money do I want to make?

2. How quickly do I want to make each promotion?

3. How many potential customers/representatives will I contact each week?

4. How many appointments will I set each week?

5. What am I going to do to generate leads?

6. How much time will I devote to training?

7. How much time do I want to devote to this business?

## *Aim–Know where you are going.*

You should know where you are going with your network marketing business. One way to establish direction is by writing a business plan. This step is often overlooked because the value of this document is not fully understood. Some people describe a business plan as a road map for doing business, I think of it more as an itinerary in which you write down your anticipated step by step process, stating what you plan to do and when you plan to do it.

A business plan is your written guide to starting and running your business successfully. Most business plans are written to convince a lending agency to lend money to the business. This is unnecessary for most network marketers because of the relatively low start-up cost for most network marketing businesses.

This does not mean you should avoid writing a business plan. As the old adage says, "Failing to plan is planning to fail." Since it serves as a written agenda for your actions and projected business time-line, it should still be regarded with the utmost importance. Just as your why helps to keep you on track, your business plan charts the course you expect to take. It is easier to know where you are going when you have a plan to get there. It does not have to be very long and professionally written. The important thing is to have one, whether it is scribbled out on a napkin or written on a piece of paper stuffed inside your wallet.

Business plans are the blueprint for how you expect to run your business. In a conventional (brick and mortar) business, the business plan defines your concept, objectives, and marketing plan. It would also cover budgeting criteria such as income projection, financing needs and financial statements, which would include cash flow and a balance sheet.

Because of the non-conventional nature of network marketing, your business plan will be structured differently than that of a conventional business. As a network marketing business owner, you may find several aspects of a conventional business plan irrelevant to your business. The format of your business plan must specifically fit you and your business. Here are some guidelines to follow when writing a business plan tailored to you as an individual.

## *Branding*

Your business plan should include establishing recognition for your business by branding yourself. Your individuality is the key to the identity of your business and a brand establishes the concept of your identity in a word or phrase. Brand recognition helps people make decisions by establishing awareness and developing trust with the consumer.

> Your individuality is the key to the identity of your business.

## *Goal Setting*

You must establish your direction and define your goals in your business plan. Remember, this is your business, and your individuality is going to be what drives it.

## *Education*

Even though most network marketers do not need a start-up loan, occasionally distributors follow this route. When a lending agency looks at a business plan to consider loaning money, they are not as interested in the size of the document as they are the content. They want to know the business owner understands his business. Be a student of your business; understand your business globally, regionally, and locally.

### Flexibility

Revisit your business plan often. It is not a static document, but rather a dynamic document. It will change with your business. Your business plan serves as a flexible itinerary, projecting where you intend your business to go and when you intend to get there. Develop contingency plans so you are prepared when changes affect your business.

When writing your business plan, do not overdo it. Be realistic and think short term projections. Use simple language because it is easily understood. Finally, identify and acknowledge your weaknesses. This will help you grow by knowing where to concentrate your learning and also how to use the strengths of others to make up for your weaknesses. Writing a business plan requires hard work and much research. When completed, it should guide you in reaching your goals.

## Fire-Take Action!

Americans are notorious for giving up what they want *most* for what they want *now*. The ideals of our society have mandated instant results in nearly everything. Citizens have been conditioned by television, fast food and the internet to expect the immediate results they believe they deserve. Although this makes for an impatient population, unwilling to work and wait for a better outcome, the idea that "good things come to those who wait" is still true.

Often people say they do not have time and cannot do more because they are already too busy. Yet many of them work their forty hours a week and go home at the end of each day, only to sit in front of the television or internet for several hours, wasting the time they could be using to build their future. You can either make excuses, or you can make money, but you cannot do both. Sometimes you must give up a good thing to have the best thing.

More than two thousand years ago a Chinese philosopher by the name of Lao Tzu said, "The journey of a thousand miles begins with the first step." Still relevant today, his wisdom can be applied to your business. Now that you have a plan, you need to put that plan in to action and make it start working for you.

Many people struggle with the issue of getting started. One thing that keeps most people from becoming a business owner is not knowing how to get started. They approach network marketing with the misconception that everything will simply fall into place, and that the machine of network marketing will carry them to their desired destination.

This lack of knowledge and blind judgment results in a great deal of confusion. People who leap before they look often find themselves in unfamiliar territory. As mentioned before, you must educate yourself about the business before you can become effective in it. Knowing how to get started is one of the keys to your effectiveness. Starting a home-based business can be a daunting task. Often a person will educate himself and still feel threatened by the unknown. This threat can intimidate a person, causing him to procrastinate and ultimately to fail to take the first step.

> You can either make excuses, or you can make money, but you cannot do both.

If network marketing is the income solution of choice, those who struggle with taking the first step may need to bolster their resolve to get started. For some, this means revisiting their why and making sure it is strong enough. Others may need to make up their mind that starting a business is what they are going to do, and just do it.

Many times, those who do take the first step struggle to follow through. They begin with zeal and enthusiasm only to be stopped at the first outset of opposition. To overcome this, they need a guide or a coach to encourage and motivate them in their business.

The need for motivation and encouragement from an outside source does not disqualify someone from being a business owner. Some people are simply unfamiliar with being their own boss. These people may eventually become the greatest network marketers ever known. They just need the right habits and principles cultivated in their lives to enable them to grow in their business.

You must have an open mind when getting started. This does not mean you should follow every whim and notion that comes your way, but be open to new ideas and concepts with which you may be unfamiliar. These new concepts often require training; therefore, you should invest in your success by continually cultivating your personal growth.

We all possess a limited quantity of time. As you begin taking action in your business, you will learn to plan your daily activities. Using a schedule gives structure to your work day and serves to measure what you accomplish. Time management is critical because time is your most valuable asset.

No one is guaranteed tomorrow, so you must work today as if it were your last. Schedule activities that help you reach your goals. By approaching your schedule with the mind-set of not having time to waste, you will prioritize your plan and eliminate unimportant activities.

Start each day with a quiet time. Find a place away from everything and everyone to hang your mental "do not disturb" sign. Take this time to read a daily devotional or to meditate, clearing your mind and aligning your thoughts to the tasks of the day. With a clear mind, you are more apt to focus on the activities that will breed success.

It is assumed, since you have decided to become a business owner that you are "in it to win." Remember, sometimes being a network marketer is a battle for survival. There are times to be on the offensive and there are times to retreat and regroup. Sometimes you have to fall back to regain momentum. Retreating is not a sign of failure but an act of strength. Those who know when to retreat, grasp the concept of survival.

Be flexible; if something is not working, change course. There are times when things move and change in your surroundings that dictate the need for you to change something about your business. It has been said that doing the same thing over and over again expecting different results is the definition of insanity.

Difficulties are going to come your way. You will not be the best you can be without some difficulties. Anyone can make excuses; you can give up, give in, quit, and live with the failure, or you can rethink your actions, learn from the mistakes and try a different approach. Your actions will be guided by your business plan and your why.

Get around people who are going places. You will find the majority of successful people have a very positive outlook. Learn to become a positive person and an encourager. As you encourage others, you will find it breeds an environment of success. Your business will not get off the ground and grow if you do not take action and get started.

# chapter 16

## mental and physical preparation

*"take the stairs" (instead of the elevator)*

**chapter 16**

# mental and physical preparation

### "take the stairs" (instead of the elevator)

### *Attention to Details*

Now that you have planned your trip and know where you want to go, the first action you should take is to prepare both mentally and physically. We say "take the stairs instead of the elevator" because, just as there must be preparation to run a marathon, in order to run a successful business there must also be measures of preparation. Some things do not come naturally. More attention must be given to areas of the business that may need improvement. These may include:

1. Public speaking

2. Talking about money

3. Selling or "Salesmanship"

4. Understanding business principles

5. Knowing the market

## Public Speaking

Most people do not enjoy speaking in public. They find it uncomfortable or frightening to make a comment, much less speak for any length of time. Public speaking requires confidence and practice. Some people may require a degree of training before they are comfortable enough to speak to a group of people in a public setting. The size of the group does not always determine the level of formality. Each particular setting naturally requires a different level of skill and/or confidence. Even speaking to someone in their home, across the dining room table, or in their living room requires confidence. There are different levels of formality in public speaking:

> It is fear that prevents most people from accomplishing something great in their lives.

1.  The ultra formal setting, such as a presidential speech.

2.  The formal, such as a seminar or lecture session.

3.  The less formal, such as small group settings in a hotel
    meeting room.

4.  The informal, such as a meeting in someone's home.

There are a number of ways you can gain the confidence to comfortably speak in public, but one element of public speaking that remains constant is the need for practice. This is one area of public speaking that you cannot cut short. For many years I heard the quote "practice makes perfect." Then I heard a variation of this quote, which says, "practice makes permanent," meaning the way you practice something, whether your form is right or wrong, is the way you will always perform it.

There is value to practicing because the more you practice something, the more proficient you will become. For example, a musician may spend hours practicing a particular arrangement for one recital, but it is the consistent practice on a regular basis that creates the musical expertise and level of proficiency the musician desires.

You can become an accomplished speaker by starting small. Volunteering to speak often in small group meetings will provide experience for you to build confidence. The fear of public speaking is only in the mind of the speaker; therefore, you must move beyond the fear and place yourself in the position to overcome it. It is fear that prevents most people from accomplishing something great in their lives.

> The more you increase your value, the more you will influence the amount of income you will make in your business.

By speaking in public and forcing yourself to overcome that fear, you can overcome fears you may have in other areas of life, which can be a catalyst for greater accomplishments. If you are going to be successful in network marketing you must overcome fear of the unknown.

Entering into a business venture can be intimidating because there is no guarantee of success. It is the fear of taking the first step that stops most people. Sometimes taking this first step means educating yourself in some areas where you lack knowledge. This can be accomplished through deliberate study of both your industry and business.

Most people who start a business already have expertise in their particular field. Many people believe they can be successful in network marketing without knowledge of the industry or marketing principles. In order to achieve the highest possible level of success, you must be willing to invest time and money to gain knowledge. Failure to do this is a common mistake with those who pursue making their fortune in network marketing.

People who do take the time to learn about network marketing increase their chances of being successful. Knowledge about network marketing does not guarantee success, nor does the lack of knowledge guarantee failure. Network marketing can be unforgiving and disappointing; however, it can also be rewarding. The difference in the outcome lies in the actions of the individual.

Some network marketers have made great sums of money by accident. Many of them have done so by recruiting others who have worked much harder than they. Although many people may feel this is wrong, it is just the nature of the business.

Most often, the three things that make a person successful in network marketing are perseverance, personality, and good marketing skills. Generally, you will need all three to become successful. The good news is, all three can be acquired and developed by anyone. With time and effort, anyone can learn how to be successful in the network marketing.

## Talking About Money

Someone who wishes to succeed in business must be able to discuss the issue of money with others. One example of this would be the acceptance of payment for services rendered. Some people are great at their area of expertise, but struggle when it comes time to request payment.

You must remember that your clients will respond to you the same way you approach them about money. If you are weak in requesting payment, they will be weak in making their payments to you. If you avoid the money issue, they will too. You must let them know up front what is expected when it comes to money, and follow through with confidence.

## Selling

There is a stigma attached to those who make their living through sales. Some sales people are pushy, arrogant, will not take no for an answer, or do not tell the truth about their product or service. This is a problem with the person, not the profession. Sales is one of the most difficult and yet rewarding professions.

Many people respond to a network marketing opportunity by saying, "I can't sell." They fail to make the connection that this is exactly what they are doing when they meet someone with whom they are interested in having a relationship or when they go for a job interview. Anyone who tells you network marketing is not selling is either ignorant or is trying to convince you to join their company, for their benefit alone.

Selling is a noble profession. Being good at selling does not require the use of high pressure and shady tactics. Finding out what customers really want is an art. The best sales people are those who understand what their clients need and want. It takes time to cultivate this skill. Once it is learned, the sky is the limit to the income you can produce. One way to become an "artist" in sales is by watching salesmen who are already good at it, and emulating them. Be careful to copy only the good qualities.

I want to emphasize that network marketing is selling! Sales is the only way products and services can make it to the consumer. There is nothing wrong with admitting this. If a person is not interested in selling, they are probably not who you are looking for as a business partner.

> It is fear that prevents most people from accomplishing something great in their lives.

Most sales people are very outgoing and have likable personalities. They are usually hard working and are what we call a "people person." These are but a few qualities to look for in a potential business partner. You should also look for people who have integrity, a good reputation, and a large circle of influence in their community.

Network marketing is not only about sales, it is also about marketing. Hence: (Network) (Marketing). "Network" is the part of the equation where you are selling or networking with other people. "Marketing" is just that: marketing your product, service, yourself, your opportunity, or anything else you desire to help you make a profit. Marketing is not sales or advertising. Advertising is only one piece of the marketing puzzle. You can have marketing without sales, but you cannot have sales without some form of marketing. You must also understand the "market" in which you do business. This is critical to knowing who will be your potential customers.

## Business Principles

No one is born with the knowledge to start and run a business. These skills must be learned and re-learned throughout your life because business environments change over time. The only way to stay current with the changes that occur in business is to continually feed the mind with information.

### Proper Nutrition

You must have proper nutrition in order to sustain life and survive. The same can be said for your business. You must feed your mind by gaining knowledge through personal study. Preparation for mental strength is accomplished by filling the pantry (your mind) with information and food for thought that can be drawn upon for decision making.

Education can begin by reading books, subscribing to periodicals and listening to audio books about your particular industry. The best information in the world is useless if it is left in a book, so buy books and read them! Feed your mind. Give yourself a fighting chance to become the best at what you do. Those who take the time to read usually experience higher levels of satisfaction than those who do not.

There are other sources of education that will help you become proficient in your business. For example, the internet contains a wealth of information, and community colleges and state universities offer classes about marketing and the internet. At times, an organization like the local chamber of commerce will provide a seminar for small business owners. The library has books available, and if all else fails, you can learn from others who are a part of your industry.

When we talk about eating right, it is not limited to just your mind. It has been said, "you are what you eat." The right kind of food will energize you, help you think clearly and make good business decisions. Do not underestimate the value your health. What good is a successful business, if you cannot enjoy the benefits of success? Why go through the struggles, just to leave it for someone else to enjoy when your life is cut short because you did not take care of it? You should live to enjoy the fruits of your labor. When educating yourself, there are several things to consider:

1.  Time necessary to dedicate yourself to study.

2.  Type of material that will be most beneficial to you.

3. Your learning style.

4. Designating funds for your education.

Many people do not have the discipline to set aside activities they enjoy, to make time for learning. Often, there are too many distractions that require their attention. It takes a strong will and perseverance to consistently study. There is reward in becoming the expert in your field. Being the expert will significantly increase your value and separate you from others in your industry. The more you increase your value, the more you will influence the amount of income you will make in your business.

When educating yourself, be careful to guard your time. Make a schedule of activities and post them in a planner or calendar. Study the areas you feel need improvement, and do not neglect your responsibilities and obligations as you pursue your education.

You do not have to know every minute detail of network marketing to be successful. The typical home-based business owner does not need to know how to do an in-depth market analysis or write a prospectus to run a successful business. For example, it is not necessary to study about inventories if you have no inventory to track. You do not need to learn about employee relations if you do not have any employees. Because the information you choose to study will influence your success, study content relevant to your home-based business.

A budget will control spending and help track purchases and investments. Budgeting also promotes and supports long-term planning which is essential to business longevity. With a budget, you can know where you stand financially at any given point in the life of your business. This helps you make educated financial decisions. There are many resources available to help you create and maintain an effective budget.

Many businesses fail within the first few years, some within the first few months, because they run out of money. Taking advantage of available tax benefits can help to reduce the financial burden on your business. There are currently over one hundred fifty tax advantages for someone who has a legitimate home-based business. "It's not how much money you make; it's how much money you keep that counts."

Discouragement is another common reason business owners fail. Sometimes being in business is overwhelming even with the right kind of motivation. Many business owners reach a point where they ask themselves if it is worth all the effort. "Staying in the game" often requires an external source of motivation. There are excellent sources for material that will help a person through rough times. Zig Ziglar, Anthony Robbins, Jim Cathcart, and others, have made careers motivating others to accomplish their goals and dreams. Investing in some of these programs can be money well spent.

In network marketing, reaching people with your message is the life blood of your business. Your knowledge of marketing will determine how many people you are going to reach. The more people you expose to your business by reaching them with your message, the more money you will make.

Learning how to effectively market your business may be your single most important pursuit. Marketing your product, service, or opportunity will never reach its potential without implementing proper marketing strategies. Many network marketers shy away from newer marketing techniques, such as marketing online, because they are uncomfortable using unfamiliar strategies.

Most network marketing companies make available written material about the company, the products or services, and the industry itself. Do not overlook this valuable resource when developing your library. Used properly, this material can help you avoid pitfalls and boost your confidence, which may increase your profits in the long term. Along with these materials, your company will provide policies and marketing suggestions. This information will help you stay within the company's guidelines and legal boundaries, which is for your protection as much as theirs.

### Exercise

Exercise is necessary for a healthy body and positive self esteem. What good is financial freedom if you do not have the health to enjoy it? Exercise has been proven to strengthen and make a person feel better. Feeling better can help to produce a better mood, which in turn, makes others around you feel better. A positive outlook can impact a negative situation to such a degree that it totally changes the outcome.

If you plan to go on a long expedition, you need to get into shape. You can accomplish this by taking the stairs instead of the elevator, parking farther away from the entrance of the places you frequent, and working out at the local gym. These routines will help you prepare physically for what you would expect to encounter on a long journey, but, you must prepare both physically and mentally.

One way to strengthen yourself mentally is by sharing with others what you have learned about your business. In network marketing, there is a great need for people who are willing to teach others. By teaching others you will gain confidence in yourself and the admiration and respect of those you help. There are many different venues in which to teach what you have learned. For example, weekly presentation meetings, conference calls, and training sessions for those who are new to your business.

Mental exercise is more often associated with business than physical exercise, yet physical exercise is still important. A person who is physically fit can better handle the stress and fatigue associated with starting and running a new business. Mental fatigue is just as real as physical, and though you may not feel like teaching, you must continue growing by using what you have learned to help others.

## The Right Mind-Set

In a survival situation the mental state of the individual is critical to his survival. The same can be said for the business owner. A great majority of people fail or quit in their business for merely psychological reasons.

Stories are told of men or women who, after being stranded in the wilderness, attributed their survival to their ability to keep a positive attitude and think clearly. Likewise, for you to survive the wiles of the economy, the obstacles of network marketing, or whatever is impeding your success, you must keep a positive attitude. One way to accomplish this is by focusing on the good things about your situation.

For example, I recently spoke with a friend of mine who is suffering from the chronic disorder fibromyalgia. This disease is characterized by pain in the muscle and connective tissues of the body. She was telling me how painful it is, and how during times of inflammation it hurts to perform normal daily activities. Apparently, regular exercise and the use of the affected muscles helps to ward off the pain. So in attempts to limit the frequency of these flair ups, she decided to begin a regimen of daily exercises.

She then told me about someone she knew who also has the same disorder. This other person gave in to the pain and would simply lie around the house all day. Her friend gained over one hundred pounds and her health steadily declined. Instead of seeing the disorder as an opportunity to get into shape and stay active and healthy, this lady surrendered to her symptoms and was losing the battle against her disorder.

This story is an example of how two different attitudes produced two very different results. One saw the good that could come from such a disorder and focused on the positive, while the other focused on the negative and became paralyzed. If a person does not respond properly in a survival situation, he can lose direction or find himself in a potentially harmful or even fatal predicament.

Preparation for unexpected circumstances is critical to survival. "Proper planning prevents poor performance!" Proper planning can make the difference between failing or staying in business. There are times when you will be confronted with circumstances you do not anticipate. This could be an unexpected financial obligation or the absence of an anticipated income. Your frame of mind will determine whether or not you respond properly.

When these situations occur, do not panic. Almost everyone is familiar with the saying, "Your attitude affects your altitude." It is no different in business. There is always one thing you can count on when running your business; that is, the unexpected. Your attitude determines your response to the unexpected. The wrong decision in your business can be fatal. In a survival situation there must be a sense of urgency. The man who responds to a critical situation with apathy will not only fail, but will affect others in the process. When the bell rings, the fireman does not finish his nap or his dinner before grabbing his suit to respond to the call.

Your chances of success in network marketing improve with every proactive and decisive action. There is a measure of risk involved in every business venture, but you must treat yours like the million dollar business it is. Anyone who invests a million dollars in his business is not going to walk away from his investment too quickly. The difference is the urgency produced by the perception that your financial freedom is at stake. This attitude can produce the sense of urgency needed to keep going in the tough times.

Urgency in action is fruitless without the right knowledge. You may be urgent about saving someone's life, but if you do not know how to administer CPR properly, it is likely the recipient of your urgency will perish. It is imperative to have knowledge about your industry and products, but more importantly you must know the proper course of actions to take in order to see the success you desire. The following ideas are very important to the success of your business:

1. Realize you are in business to make a profit.

2. Recognize the value in small steps.

3. Do not expect to make a million dollars the first year!

4. Be in business for the "long-haul."

5. What do you want on your tombstone?

Many people fail to remember they started their business to make a profit. They fail to make decisions that keep them on track with their budget and business plan. One of the most common mistakes business owners make is too many purchases and financial commitments early in the life of their business. When I was young, we seldom, if ever, ate meals outside the home. I do not remember eating out other than on vacation or some other special occasion. When we did eat out, dad would say, "Don't let your eyes be bigger than your stomach." He was referring to the amount of food we thought we could eat.

Applying this to business, everyone wants the newest computer and the fanciest desk or office. They pursue the trappings of success without their balance sheet backing it up. This mistake overloads the cash flow and nothing is left for unexpected expenses. It is wiser to wait until your business is established to buy the nicer, fancier, and newer. Use what you have now, and upgrade as your business grows and your income can support such purchases.

The idea of taking small steps when starting out eludes many new representatives. A Highway Patrol officer will tell you that the faster a car is traveling, the more devastating the accident. This also applies to business. Taking smaller steps prevents larger accidents because the consequences of errors are less devastating. For a fledgling business, this could mean the difference between success and failure.

On a more personal level, many people get so "wrapped up" in their business, they forget to take time to enjoy life. Enjoying life is supposed to be the purpose for financial freedom anyway. Keep your business in perspective by taking time for family and friends; you'll be glad you did!

> Urgency in action is fruitless without the right knowledge.

Many new distributors believe they are going to make a million dollars in their first year. Though there is nothing wrong with dreaming big, you must not overlook reality. I am not saying it cannot happen. It has before, and it will again; however, it is not the norm. Do not discourage yourself or set yourself up for failure by setting unrealistic goals. Be sensible about the goals you set for yourself. When you reach a particular goal, you can celebrate and move to the next level.

Start your business with the commitment to see it through to the end. Do not start if you are not in it for the "long-haul." If you do not take your business seriously, no one else will either. This is your business, not theirs. If you opened a store front in your town, and someone walked in and said, "You'll never make a living doing this, and if I were you I would quit," would you listen to them? Certainly not! You would not take financial advice from those who are broke, so do not listen to those who are not business owners.

Believe in yourself and your abilities because you have what it takes to be successful in network marketing. You have a unique perspective of your business. Regardless of what others might think, this point of view is of great value. Take advantage of it and make it work for you. Do not allow limitations in your thinking. Never tell yourself, "I can't do that," or, "They will never come into my business," or, "I don't have the time to run a business." All of these are limitations you place upon yourself. Limiting yourself will limit your income and ultimately your freedom.

What do you want on your tombstone? I'm not talking about pizza; I'm talking about the idea of leaving a legacy. This concept is foreign to most people because they think leaving a legacy is only for presidents or someone who has more money than they can count. Everyone should think seriously about how he wants to be remembered. How do you want to be remembered? Is it how much money you made, or how many people you helped? Considering your legacy will help you determine how to live.

Finally, have fun! Laugh at yourself. Do not take yourself too seriously. This is just as important as any other aspect of your business. Control what you can; don't worry about the rest. Optimistic people go further, have more fun, live longer, and make more friends! Avoid pessimism. Negative people are always negative, so stay away from them. Have a positive mental attitude, approach, outlook

> Start your business with the commitment to see it through to the end.

and mind-set. People will respond to your business the same way you approach them. Eating and exercising properly will prepare you for the road ahead.

# chapter 17

## take others with you

*"it's a team effort"*

# chapter 17

# take others with you

### *"it's a team effort"*

When my beautiful wife and I were first married, we enjoyed camping and hiking together in the mountains. Many times we would go for a day hike or camp overnight. Over the years, we have taken many trips all over the United States and Mexico. We have been in all but a few of the states. Our favorite places to visit are out west, in Wyoming and Montana.

We enjoyed traveling more because we were together. The trips would have been pretty boring had either one of us been alone. There is a sense of adventure when you travel with others because they see things differently than you do, which makes the experience even better.

Whether hunting, hiking, or in business, the journey can be more pleasant when you have someone with you. Business is not necessarily about pleasure, but it does not have to be without pleasant times. The old saying goes, "You should not mix business with pleasure." On the contrary, doing business should be a pleasure. You should enjoy both your work and being around those with whom you work.

If you are open-minded, you will realize other people have much to offer when it comes to running a business. Many times these people may not be interested in leading, but may have great ideas on how to accomplish different tasks. They also help to broaden your view of how things can work, which will benefit everyone. "Many hands make light work" is a quote my pastor makes from time to time. Do not overlook the potential encouragement and ideas that could help your business reach higher levels by including others.

> You should enjoy both your work and being around those with whom you work.

While there are some who are not interested in taking a leadership role, there are those who have the qualities necessary to help things run smoothly. There is always a need for people to "step up to the plate" and take responsibility. Anyone who understands his business can help train those who may not. When a new person joins your business, he must be trained. This is an area where those who are willing can be of service. In network marketing, there are several areas in which a person can make himself useful.

1. Training

2. Organizing

3. Presentations

4. Mentoring

5. Facilitating

Training one person does not require a great deal of time or effort, but it does require someone who knows what he is talking about. There are people in your organization that can pass their knowledge on to others who come into your business. There are some people who may not have the desire to stand in front of the group to do a presentation, but would be glad to help someone with one-on-one training. Do not get so wrapped up in training that you leave other important activities undone. Remember, training is an on-going process. No one learns everything they need to know about their business in the first training session.

There are those who are unwilling to speak in front of a group, but have the organizational skills to prepare for a meeting. They can help set up the room or work at the welcoming table, handing out name tags and registering visitors.

You will find people who enjoy doing presentations in front of a group. These are the people who, more than likely, have a larger circle of influence and are accustomed to the attention that accompanies a large group setting. Often this person is a "Type A" personality. You can benefit greatly from this type of personality, but they are usually not as teachable as others may be in your business.

Not all "Type A" personalities are comfortable speaking in public. A person who is comfortable speaking in front of a large group can certainly make your job a lot easier. Having someone in your organization willing to work and carry some of the load is more valuable than you may think. Take advantage of the willingness and talents of others.

> Being a mentor is one of the most important roles a person can fill.

Being a mentor is one of the most important roles a person can fill. Mentoring is much more involved than training. As a mentor, you accept a measure of responsibility for the future of that person. Mentoring is a powerful practice that ensures a new member of your organization gets the training and development he needs and deserves.

Many new distributors drop out after a short period of time because they are not properly mentored. Taking the time to mentor new representatives will give them confidence and security. A person who is mentored develops a stronger resolve to stay in the business when things get tough. Having a mentoring program as an integral part of your business practices will result in a stronger organization.

A facilitator is the person who may open the meeting by welcoming the visitors, introducing the guest speaker, giving a testimony, or making announcements. It is important that someone other than the person giving the presentation open the meeting and introduce the speaker. This gives credibility to the speaker and makes for a more persuasive presentation.

Having a facilitator provides an opportunity for other representatives to participate in the meeting. This involvement gives those who are not yet ready to do a full presentation a way to build confidence. It also breaks the monotony of the meeting for the visitors who may be in attendance.

Allowing and encouraging others to participate shows prospective representatives that it is a team effort and there is something special taking place. This activity legitimizes your business in their eyes when they see different people, from different walks of life, actively participating in this venture. Recognizing the team effort will encourage them to become a participant as well.

It is important to have some structure in place for training, mentoring, and developing people in your business. As your team grows, there will be more people to share duties and responsibilities, but you must remember, you are a leader, not a manager.

If you do not provide this support and structure yourself, at the very least find a good source to which you can direct your people. Once they are competent, they can provide support and structure for others in their organization. Collaborating in this role can be beneficial because many people do not have the time, energy, knowledge, or patience to establish training and support material.

You must learn the importance of investing your time in the right kind of people. The right kind of person desires to make a difference in his life and in the lives of others. Proverbs 27:17 says *"Iron sharpeneth iron; so a man sharpeneth the countenance of his friend."* This ancient proverb reveals the wisdom of King Solomon which you can apply to the value of a business partner.

Nearly all network marketers venture into business by themselves and rightly should. You should find a person you trust who is like minded, with which to simply share ideas, thoughts and counsel. The way you develop your skills often determines how well your business will do. Therefore, if you have someone to help you learn and develop your skills; the result of the whole can be greater than the sum of its parts.

When logging in the woods, the lumberjack knows two mules yoked together can collectively pull more than two mules pulling individually. This is called synergy. The same concept applies to the business world and is used regularly in corporate America. Much can be said about finding the right business partner. For some, this will mean going into business together, yet for others it will simply be a friend who will be an encouragement.

## Become a Leader

Natural leadership is a characteristic possessed by very few, however, it is a quality that can be developed. People who desire to become a leader can learn and grow into leadership roles. War has demonstrated time and again that some of the greatest leaders are the common man forged in the fires of necessity. People who are born with the natural ability to command a following of men are few and far between.

> Many who have become the greatest leaders in history were common men faced with uncommon danger and overwhelming odds.

Many who have become the greatest leaders in history were common men faced with uncommon danger and overwhelming odds. These men gained freedom for our nation and won the wars that have kept the world, for the most part, free from tyranny for more than two hundred years.

To become a true leader, you must become informed. The old adage, "leaders are readers" is true. Reading does not guarantee that you will become a leader, but those who read are usually leaders in their field of expertise. There are many books available that deal with the subject of leadership. You should obtain a few of them for your personal development library. A leader has qualities that stand out above the rest. A few of these qualities are listed below. A good leader...

### 1.    Is a good listener.

People express their emotions, needs, wants and desires through verbal communication. When a baby cries, the mother who is attuned to the different cries of her child can discern if it is a cry of pain or hunger. Friends often lean on each other for support; a friend who provides a listening ear is often considered a very dear friend. One of the most common grievances wives have against their husbands is that they do not listen.

Human beings are by nature social creatures, and that social factor dictates the necessity of communication. In any relationship, there is a need for understanding which can only be established by listening.

Listening endears the husband to the wife, the mother to the child and the leader to his followers. A leader who listens is able to more effectively lead and help those who follow.

Sometimes, this includes listening to what is not spoken. Many times it is the ability to "read between the lines" that proves to be more important than hearing what is being said. A distributor may approach their upline to share a "concern" about another distributor. A good leader who is discerning may understand the situation and recognize the malevolence and act accordingly. In network marketing, it is to your advantage to have good listening skills.

Listening seems to be a lost art in our society. Everything we may need or want to communicate can be transmitted electronically. Whether it be by texting on cell phones, e-mailing, or messaging in social media, time is not always taken to insure the correct message is being delivered. In doing so, we are losing some of the meaning and beauty of verbal communication. When the interaction takes place electronically, there is a disconnect in the conversation and when the listening stops the communication diminishes.

In order to effectively communicate, you must first become a good listener. Regardless of how "progressive" society may become, there will never be a complete substitute for verbal communication. Speaking, and listening, will always be the preferred method of communicating. Therefore, a good leader must be a good listener as it is key to understanding the needs and desires of those he serves.

**2. Is interested in the success of others.**

The person who cares only about himself rarely gains any significant following. Most people can discern when a person is genuinely interested in them. True interest in the success of others is important in gaining influence, especially to the network marketer who is just starting his business. Showing an interest in the lives of other people can promote successful communication. When you know that a person is truly interested in your success, it is easier to take that person more seriously.

**3. Is patient.**

Patience is truly a virtue when it comes to leadership. A good leader realizes that different people are at different stages in life. He recognizes there are different levels of education, business success, relationships and personal development, and works patiently to help everyone grow as much as possible in every area.

## 4. Is creative.

The leader who understands the complexities of business, will have the insight to use creative strategies to help his organization grow. Pablo Picasso once said, "Every act of creation is first of all an act of destruction." Though it may sound enigmatic and philosophical, it is a truth many leaders learn and develop. Creativity is the fuel that keeps the engine of new ideas running.

> A good leader recognizes the positive attributes of people and helps them build on those qualities.

Business environments are constantly changing. Status quo marketing and promoting is business suicide. In order to develop creative marketing and promoting, a good leader must first destroy the conventional dogmas and approach the subject with a fresh clean slate.

## 5. Knows when to have fun.

Work does not have to be a drag. A good leader can make the business fun and exciting. There are many different ways to accomplish this. Each organization has its own personality because it takes on the characteristics of its leaders. As a leader, you should help others enjoy working their business.

## 6. Knows how to motivate people.

One of the most important responsibilities of a leader is to motivate those in his downline. This motivation is essential to keeping the distributors active in the business. There are at least three kinds of people in any organization, underachievers, average achievers, and overachievers. You must learn to balance incentives and encouragement to keep all three motivated.

Overachievers often become very successful in their business, because they are internally motivated. When you show your willingness to work with everyone, regardless of their level of success, you will be seen as more genuine.

**7.   Knows how to earn the trust of others.**

This is accomplished by first, never talking negatively about someone else, and secondly keeping your word. If these two principles are broken, it will destroy any trust you have established. Others know if you will talk about someone else in a negative way, you will also talk negatively about them. If you do not follow through with what you promise, people who are interested in your business will see you as disingenuous and your business opportunity as a sham.

**8.   Dispels fears by displaying confidence.**

Many times in network marketing, things do not go as planned. It is necessary for you as a good leader to dispel fears by displaying confidence in your downline and in your business plan and model. Every business has its ups and downs. You must convey a positive attitude in the critical moments. The wise leader dispels their fears of personal development and addresses their struggles, showing that he truly cares about their success.

**9.   Recognizes qualities in other people.**

Many people only see their own abilities and qualities. In our society, people are quick to point out the faults and failures in others. A good leader recognizes the positive attributes of people and helps them build on those qualities.

**10.   Builds on the positive.**

People naturally look to the leader for guidance and advice. In network marketing, people do not initially follow a business model; they follow other people. Because the leader is looked to, he will also be looked up to.

It is a great honor and responsibility when others follow in your footsteps. The amount of influence you will have on your organization is in direct proportion to your level of honesty and integrity. By demonstrating these qualities, you make it easier for those who follow you.

Leaders are also open-minded. They realize there may be more than one approach to reaching the same goal. People we would label as narrow-minded are rarely open to suggestions. They, like the horse wearing blinders, only see what they want to when they turn their head in that direction.

Trust your instincts. There will be times when you are not sure what to do. Make your decision and then stand behind that decision. Have confidence in your abilities. The courage to do what it takes (to prevent being trampled by the Moose) comes from within.

# chapter 18

## the right equipment

*"use a hammer, not your shoe"*

# chapter 18

# the right equipment

*"use a hammer, not your shoe"*

In the wilderness of a Moose economy there are many destinations and a great number of trails to get you there. It is easy to get lost if you are not prepared and do not have the gear fitted for survival. To make your trip successful, you should make yourself aware of all the tools available and take the steps necessary to learn how to implement them in your journey.

Just as you would carry a backpack on a hiking trip, you should have a backpack on your journey through the wilderness of the Moose economy. The pack I am speaking of is your knowledge base of your business and marketing skills. Packing this "backpack" is not as easy as it may seem. There are a number of details that will govern what to take and how to arrange them in your pack.

No one can determine how to pack your things better than you. You are responsible for carrying it, so its weight and value will be determined by what items you include and where, how and when you use them. The items you pack reveal your level of preparation for the wilderness. The order in which you pack these items will show your priorities for the journey.

You would be foolish to disregard all the available tools and set out unprepared. As a network marketer, you will need to develop and gather tools and equipment such as working capital, information and education, marketing tools and strategies, and metaphorically speaking, a first aid kit for times of difficulty or distress.

Webster's Dictionary defines marketing as "1 a: the act or process of selling or purchasing in a market. b: the process or technique of promoting, selling, and distributing a product or service. 2: an aggregate of functions involved in moving goods from producer to consumer."

Since network marketing is your income solution of choice, it is wise to know and understand how to actually market your products and services, your business, and yourself. Statistically, more than 90% of all representatives in network marketing quit within the first several months of their venture. Some simply give up because they lose interest, run out of money, or do not know how to market their products or services. Others fail to recognize that they now own a business. The employee mind-set is so ingrained into them they cannot grasp the magnitude of all that is required of a business owner. They have tried to watch others and emulate the actions of those who are successful without fully understanding the principles driving their success.

> In the wilderness of a Moose economy there are many destinations and a great number of trails to get you there.

Granted, there are some who see greater measures of success more quickly than others. The reason often cited for this quick success is the size of their circle of influence. This is a reasonable explanation to the new representative, but when they begin to understand the opportunity to enlarge their circle of influence by taking advantage of modern marketing tools, such reasoning becomes less valid.

For the remaining majority to increase their chances of success, they must learn, understand and utilize the marketing techniques of the contemporary marketplace. This section is not designed to teach the ins and outs of every available avenue of marketing, but to help you discover new and exciting ways to draw people to your product, your service, and yourself and, ultimately, to increase your income.

These are the "nuts-and-bolts" of marketing strategies. These topics will provide information from which you can develop sound solutions to get your business in front of the right people. These areas will not be covered in detail, as it would be too lengthy for this format. My hope is that this will give you enough information to start you in the right direction. It will be up to you to carry through with more research and ultimately implement what you have learned. I have chosen carefully the topics I feel are the most relevant and will have the most impact on your business.

As mentioned in other parts of the book, the first action a person must take is to get started. Fear of the unknown is a strong deterrent. This concept may sound simple, but it is this very step that stops most people who are given the opportunity to start a business. If you are struggling to make that first step due to your fear, to overcome this fear, your first step may need to be returning the phone call to the person who introduced you to network marketing, or, attending a business presentation meeting with a friend who is already pursuing their dreams through network marketing. It is this first action that helps you build momentum in the right direction.

> Statistically, more than 90% of all representatives in network marketing quit within the first several months of their venture.

As you read through this list, remember that the goal is to get into and stay in the forefront of your customers minds. These are simply listed in alphabetical order for ease of reference; the order in which they appear has no bearing on their level of importance to your business. Some of these tools and techniques date back more than five hundred years, while others are considered cutting edge.

Regardless of their age, each one can still serve some capacity in you marketing strategy. Before implementing any of these into your business, be sure to consult your company's policies concerning the use and restrictions of various marketing venues. Following this list, you will learn how people search for and find information, how someone grows by using that information, and finally, what you are responsible to do with what you know.

# Marketing Tools

## Autoresponders

An autoresponder is an automatic e-mail reply sent to a person that requested specific information via an e-mail inquiry. Autoresponders can be set up to give either a simple "Thank you for your interest..." response, or more complex responses such as sending an e-book or report of some kind. Autoresponders are more often the tool of choice for those seeking to gain e-mail addresses, phone numbers, names, or other information, to build a contact list for marketing campaigns.

> A carefully crafted series of follow-up e-mails can produce a dramatic increase in sales.

The more common autoresponders are called sequential autoresponders. A sequential autoresponder cannot only send an immediate reply to an e-mail inquiry, but it can also send additional information at regularly scheduled intervals. A carefully crafted series of follow-up e-mails can produce a dramatic increase in sales.

There are several ways the autoresponder can be useful in your business. One way is by sending regularly scheduled messages to representatives who need to be kept up to date, which is a critical part of motivating your team. It can also be used for sending information about your business to prospects interested in learning more about a solution to their income needs.

The autoresponder can be used to send material to people who have subscribed to information you are selling or giving away. Regardless of your purpose for using it, the autoresponder is great because it is an automated process which frees up your time for other activities.

## Blogging

As the Web 2.0 concept took root and began to spread, there were several new innovative ideas for internet-based social interaction that began to emerge. Of these, the "blog," a contraction of the words "web log," began to increase in popularity. The blog is a simple electronic online diary that is posted by an individual in chronological order. It is not as complex as a website but is very useful in the distribution of information and ideas. A blog is best related to a traditional newspaper. Within its content are often pictures, messages, ideas, news, information, videos, and even advertisements.

There are basically two types of blog pages; personal and corporate. Personal blogs usually contain events and thoughts that are posted to a page for the same purpose a person would keep a written diary. The blog, however, is posted for anyone who has access to read the content.

Corporations use blogging as a source of marketing media to announce new products or gain feedback through forums made available on their site. This method of social media marketing has proven effective for many companies. As a network marketing entrepreneur, you will also find blogging to be a very useful tool in recruiting and sharing your business opportunity or income solution.

Blogs can give a personal touch to your internet marketing that people will connect with immediately. Your personality portrayed through your blog will help you produce a following of people that want to keep up with what is going on in your life and business. This following of people then becomes the seed for a new "warm market" for your business.

A blog can be easily used to engage your key audience by delivering information relevant to their interests. Followers can subscribe to blogs and in most cases participate by leaving comments about recent posts. Blogging is one of the few ways to give a human face and voice to your business.

There are many business uses of the blog. Knowledge is power. Having the right information is the key to knowledge; therefore, information is one of the most important commodities found on the internet. Increased traffic by having the "right" information on your blog will yield better results in the search engines, ultimately translating into more visitors and more sales for you.

## Business Cards

With a little creativity, this promotional tool can prove to be very effective. Business cards usually contain the company name, contact information, sometimes a byline about the company such as the motto or short mission statement. A network marketer should always have a good supply of business cards readily available to give out at a moment's notice. The business card can be posted to a community bulletin board, in barber shops and grocery stores. They are also useful when attending a networking meeting with other local business owners.

## Business Presentation Meetings

There is always an energy and level of excitement generated when numbers of people gather in numbers. A weekly business presentation meeting is essential to network marketing businesses because it allows the representatives to gather with like minded business owners. These meetings are valuable because they can be used to accomplish many different things in a direct sales atmosphere. Weekly business presentation meetings are often used to inform prospects about the business opportunity, showing them what is involved and giving them a feel of the business. These meetings can also be used for coaching and training sessions to educate the distributors.

## Capture Pages

Capture pages are critical elements in attraction marketing. The object of the capture page is to "capture" the viewers' attention and contact information. The content of the capture page is designed to "connect" with the viewers. Once the connection is made, they are drawn into a series of multiple and/or gradually higher-priced purchases by first providing relevant information, then offering an e-book or promotional item of value, at low or no cost.

Once the viewer decides to accept the free offer or to purchase the low cost promotional item, the viewer is required to enter minimal vital information. Capture pages vary as the information they "capture" differs to suit the marketing needs of the business owner. These pages will collect marketing information like the name, e-mail address, phone number, etc. of the viewer (now prospect). This information can then be used in conjunction with autoresponders to to follow-up with the contact and "pitch" other items to the prospect for further purchases.

## ClickBank

ClickBank is an affiliate marketing service that allows you to earn a commission on a variety of web-based services and products. Once you become a member, you can browse through the available categories to choose what product or service you want to promote. Once you have chosen the product and begin to produce sales, you are paid a commission on each sale. You can also sell your products and services, as long as they are electronically transmittable.

## Conference Calls

Found to be useful by those in the business world, conference calls have been adopted by network marketers to educate both active and potential representatives alike. This method of communication can prove useful for a number of different activities. The dynamic conference call, with guest speakers and well structured agendas, can encourage potential business partners to take the next step of joining you in your business by answering many of their questions even before they have been asked. They can also be useful in training new representatives in company and product information, and in marketing techniques.

## Direct Mail

Also known as mass mailing, this medium is used to generate sales, spread the word about your company or product, provide educational newsletters to establish credibility and authority, give discounts and send greetings or thank you cards to loyal customers. Some people think using direct mail is a thing of the past, but it can actually be a very integral part of your business. You can use direct mail to promote your website, but use this service wisely since direct mail can be somewhat expensive.

## E-books

If you are knowledgeable about your business, you may consider writing and using e-books to get your information into people's hands. E-books are basically any document formatted as a book that can be transmitted electronically. The most popular format for e-books is the Adobe PDF (portable document format.)

## E-zines

A good way to establish yourself as an authority is through the use of e-zine articles. These are basically electronic magazine articles. Similar to magazine articles, these online articles establish the author as an authority, but to a much larger possible audience.

> A good way to establish yourself as an authority is through the use of e-zine articles.

The key to success with e-zines is to become popular in the e-zine sites through good copywriting. (The use of words to make your business appealing to consumers) If your content is well written and relevant to the masses, you can develop a substantial following. If you have done a good job of establishing yourself as the expert in your industry, you can place a dollar value on the information you provide, and make it available for purchase. Your following can generate a steady income for you as they buy what you have to offer.

## Forums

These online discussion sites are widely used by people who have an interest or opinion about a predetermined topic. This is another online outlet for business owners to establish themselves as the expert.

## Keywords

Keywords are the words and phrases that people use when they are conducting a search on the internet. The words they use to search for something are tracked by search engines, and complex algorithms are used to determine which websites to select in subsequent searches. These algorithms are a closely guarded secret with the search engine companies.

The algorithms are used to determine the popularity of web pages, which determines page rankings and search results. All keywords carry a certain value with the various search engines. It is important to understand which keywords the search engines regard as valuable pertaining to the theme of your site. This will determine which keywords you should use, and how you incorporate them into your website.

## Leads

Leads are the life blood of your business. Leads are prospects that have shown an interest in what you have to offer. A lead usually consists of a name and contact information, such as a phone number or e-mail address. There are many ways to obtain leads. You can purchase "leads lists" from "leads list providers" on the internet. Be cautious when purchasing these lists, because many times a list is sold and used and resold and reused by many different people.

One of the best ways to generate a leads list is to gather the information yourself using your website. If you have an e-book with unique information about your product, service, or business, you can offer it using a capture page as mentioned earlier. The capture page will generate a list of prospects that show an interest in what you have. This list is kept by you and should be used by you only. You can then use that list to focus your marketing efforts. Typically, those already interested in what you are offering are more likely to purchase from you.

## Magazine Articles

Another form of the printed word, when used correctly, this media tool commands the attention of a very exclusive demographic. You may at some point feel inclined to contribute a column to a network marketing industry specific magazine, which would give you credibility with readers and, thereby, bring you one step closer to your goal of becoming the expert in your field.

## Merchant Accounts

If you desire to build a website designed to receive payments for services or products, you must have what is called a merchant account. There are companies that provide this service on the web. You will need a merchant account to process credit cards, and electronic check payments. Once you have an account established, make certain you follow all the rules very closely. It may be wise to establish several accounts at once. This way, if you have a problem with one account, you can easily switch over to another.

## Newspapers

The printed word has wielded its power since before the discovery of electricity. Declared to be responsible for the rise and fall of world powers, this tool is still very potent and should not to be overlooked.

## Pay-Per-Click Advertising

This is the internet's counterpart to billboards. Just as people see a billboard as they travel the highways, internet surfers are presented with a barrage of these miniature and often animated placards of persuasion. Pay per-click ads are an internet based advertising tool used on web pages where advertisers pay for advertising only when their ad is clicked.

The top three providers of this service are Google, Yahoo, and Microsoft. This tool is effective and popular because it allows for mass visibility on a limited budget. One benefit to using this model is how quickly you can have an ad campaign up and running. In a matter of minutes, you can have your advertisements working and many times have immediate response from visitors as well.

### Podcasting/Videocasting

The days of the media empire, consisting of television, radio, newspapers and magazines are all but passé. With the advent and acceptance of internet-based media, you can now get a message to whomever you want, free! Two widely used internet technologies are podcasting and videocasting.

Podcasting allows the user to record an audio message and upload the saved file to the internet. Anyone interested in obtaining that recording can then download the file directly to their mp3 player. Done properly, this is an incredibly useful tool when trying to promote a book or event. Simply send an e-mail message or update your social media status with the link, have your podcast ready for delivery, and you are the next media craze. With advancements in technology, you are now able to hook up your video camera to your computer, record a video message, and upload it to the internet for the whole world to see.

If videocasting is something you will use on a regular basis in your business, it may be wise to invest in better than average equipment. No one likes to see or hear poor quality. Those who have a website for their business can also offer a series of audio files to share information about their business, company or industry. This is a very effective tool to educate large numbers of followers and create awareness of a product or service.

### Radio

Like television, this media outlet never stops. By capturing the imagination of the listeners, this marketing tool can produce very impressive results on both a local and national level. Some talk show hosts are open to having local guests on for interviews. This would be a great way to gain exposure for network marketing in your local area. When dealing with this type of media, you must be careful to stay within the bounds of your company policies.

### RSS / Web Feeds

The nature of social media lends itself very well to a method of information updating called "Really Simple Syndication" or RSS. When this term is used, it is more commonly referred to as "RSS Feeds." This is making reference to the formats used to publish frequently updated information from sources such as blog entries, news updates, videos, and audio recordings.

This tool is very useful when you have an announcement or notice you want to send to your organization or your potential prospects for your business opportunity. RSS feeds are also very useful when monetizing your website or providing content that is valuable to the people who may be following you as the expert in your network marketing business. RSS feeds give you the power of immediate updates to all your followers at the same time.

## Shopping Cart

The shopping cart is the face of your merchant account, and is the tool customers will use to view items they are ready to purchase, process orders, and check the status of previously purchased items. The more tools and user-friendly features you make available to your customers, the better their experience. If their purchase was secure, fast, easy to understand, and proved to be an enjoyable experience overall, they will not only return for future purchases, but more than likely will tell others about your site.

If your shopping cart is hard to understand and has few features, they may go somewhere else without making a purchase. There are several different shopping cart software providers available on the web. Not all shopping cart software will fit your needs and efficiently process your sales. Since everyone's requirements are different, research will help you find the shopping cart service that best suites your needs.

## Social Media

While the electronic bulletin board was the forerunner to the internet and gained quite a substantial following, with the advent of the internet, things have changed very rapidly. Forums (discussion boards) and chat rooms sprang up almost immediately. This was the real reason the internet was so broadly received.

The ability to share opinions and files began rising. Bulletin boards, and later, chat rooms and forums, are where social media started. Now social media is used broadly in business for everything from messaging to search engine optimization. Social media is simply an internet media format used to convey important information relevant to the common interests of many people.

For any business to thrive it must connect with its customers, and prospects. Through social networking sites, businesses are able to listen and interact with their target market.

## Telephone

There is a difference between marketing on the telephone and telemarketing. Telemarketing is the act of arbitrarily calling leads lists and referrals in attempts to market a product, service or opportunity. Telephone marketing is contacting pre-qualified contacts to market your business, product or service. A pre-qualified contact is someone you already know (your warm market) or someone who contacts you requesting information about your business.

## Television

Unequalled by any other media source, this giant of media has proven to be powerful in marketing and advertising through commercials and infomercials. Advertising on television can be very expensive, but there are some local cable shows that you may find useful and fairly inexpensive. When dealing with this type of media, you must be careful to stay within the bounds of your company policies.

## Trade Shows and Job Fairs

Trade shows and job fairs are organized events created in local communities for the purpose of giving exposure to companies desiring to attract potential clients or prospective employees. Most community centers of larger cities host at least two of these events per year; some cities schedule them more often. The cost associated with participating in this type of event can range from less than one hundred dollars to several hundred. For the network marketer, these events can be a very useful recruiting tool and in gaining a presence in you local community.

### Web-based Business Tools

Google, Yahoo, and Microsoft are more than just search engines. They have developed a number of tools to help you with your web-based business in the area of productivity and marketing through the use of banners, analytics, etc. While these three are the largest, there are other companies that provide web based tools which may prove useful in your business.

### Website

Web pages and search engines have been around almost as long as the internet. A web page is a unique electronic advertisement that distinguishes one company, institution, family, business, or other entity from another by graphics, word content, and layout. Visitors are invited to view the website and therefore gain something from its use. A website can also be designed to allow a viewer to purchase goods or services from the owner of the site.

## Marketing Methods

### Affiliate Marketing

Amazon is perhaps the initiator of the concept of affiliate programs on the web. They started this phenomenon by allowing other people to promote Amazon's products on their individual website. Once you become an affiliate of Amazon, you can promote a featured product and get paid a commission on the sale. This method of producing an income has been duplicated all over the internet, and grown into a separate industry of its own. There are several good affiliate programs offered on the web. The key to effective affiliate marketing is having a very high value-to-price ratio. The most important asset in affiliate programs is the content of the wordcopy being offered.

### Direct Marketing

This form of marketing is also known as response marketing. Direct marketing is used when a marketer sends an advertisement directly to a specific person or group of people and conveys a very specific "call to action." This call to action can be responded to by visiting a website, calling a phone number, or sending an e-mail to the marketer. While there are many different forms of direct marketing, both traditional and internet based, the most common is what some people refer to as "junk mail." This mail is typically used by local merchants or national chain stores to advertise specials or promotions.

### E-mail Marketing

Since the advent of the internet, people have been sending messages electronically. This form of sending letters and communicating over a network proves effective in promoting business. Using this method of marketing can prove to be very useful in building your network marketing business; however, because everyone hates getting those pesky unsolicited advertising e-mails (more often referred to as spam), you should be careful when launching an e-mail marketing campaign.

Improperly sending mass e-mails can result in you being classified as a "spammer" which can result in you being blacklisted with the major ISP's. In the world of major e-mail providers, once you have been blacklisted, you can no longer reach your intended audience through e-mail. There are guidelines that should be strictly followed. I recommend that you use a hosted service rather than your software. Hosted services have already established credibility and can handle the load often generated by e-mail campaigns. It is much cheaper to pay a hosting service than to buy the equipment and do it yourself. The goal is to remain a legitimate e-mail sender with the main ISPs. You should also use opt-in and opt-out models that are easily understood by the end user.

### Internet Marketing

In less than two decades, the internet has become the vehicle of choice for advertising and transferring information and is the new crucial media to get your message to the masses. Business owners who ignore the shift in our society toward the internet will find themselves looking for a "career" rather than a "market."

Through the internet, anyone can easily promote his business to millions of people at once. Imagine what this could do for someone desiring to promote his network marketing business. Through internet marketing, the message of your income solution can take the spotlight, and your personality can increase your circle of influence.

When using the internet as a marketing tool, you should determine who you desire to reach with your message. You must make an effort to reach only your desired target audience. Your message is powerless if it is reaching the wrong group of people, no matter how large that group may be.

Not everyone wants what you have to offer. This concept cuts against the grain of many network marketers' rhetoric. If you understand and accept this fact, you will be much more efficient in marketing your business. Your valuable time and resources are best used when reaching only people that are interested in being a network marketing business owner.

### *Referral Marketing*

Word of mouth has always been one of the most powerful and sought after forms of advertising. Referral marketing and strategic reciprocal links are the "next generation" of word of mouth on the internet. Many websites already have a following (an online warm market). When two websites add links to each other they in essence expand their warm market by endorsing each other with these reciprocal links. A strategic link is a link placed with other sites that are not in competition with you, but that complement your business offer. This increases the number of hits and traffic through your site, which helps your ranking in the search engines.

These are not all the available marketing tools, but if you understand and use a few of these, you will be off to a good start. Do not limit yourself to the use of just one. Different combinations of various techniques can prove very successful. At the same time, it is not necessary to do everything at once. It takes time to learn, apply and master each technique, so give yourself time to adjust and become adept.

You must use the methods that best suit your needs. Then, just as if you were to put them into your backpack, adopt them as yours and use them at the appropriate times. A balanced pack will help you be more sure footed as you accumulate and utilize certain skills, strategies, and tools for your journey along the trail of the Moose economy. The way you arrange them in your business will determine your priorities and preparedness for what lies ahead.

## *Searching and Finding*

It is no secret that I like to hunt big game. I grew up hunting with my dad. He taught me to respect game animals and never shoot anything I did not plan to eat, no matter how small the animal. Many times, when he would come home from work, we would hike into the woods and very quietly slip into a strategic position for a shot at a squirrel.

If deer were in season, we would go to some of his favorite spots in the area where he grew up. We always had a good time, even when we did not see any deer. In winter, we would track rabbits in the snow. Somehow he always knew how old the tracks were.

When I was a little older, we had the opportunity to hunt deer in South Texas and antelope in Wyoming. I have also enjoyed taking my son as he was growing up. I will certainly cherish these memories as long as I live.

Hunting for big game is not easy. There is a lot of preparation in studying the habitat and habits of the animal. Contrary to popular belief, it takes skill, patience, and a little luck to be a successful big game hunter. A difficult part of hunting is being invisible to the game. This is much harder than many people realize. If someone was sitting in your living room when you came home from work, would you not notice?

When hunting, you must often search for the spot you believe will yield the best results. You must be aware of your surroundings and be able to read the "signs." Understanding your environment is essential to a successful search. Realizing there are people who have gone before you who have insight and experience crucial to your success is of utmost importance. This concept also applies to your business!

There are people all around you who are looking for a way to produce additional income. Because of the Moose economy, people are more open minded to suggestions of unique and unconventional income solutions. They are looking for information that is relative to their needs and personal goals. Many are searching for something to help them through these rough financial times, retirement, or both.

> There are people all around you who are looking for a way to produce additional income.

For you to be successful in your network marketing business, you need to know what kind of people are searching for extra income. This information can guide you in your marketing efforts. There are several categories of people who are looking for additional income. They are as follows:

1. People being laid off from their job.

2. People who have recently lost investments.

3. People desiring more freedom.

4. People simply wanting to reach a financial goal.

5. People who have a desire to be their own boss.

There are many people who have fallen victim to our wild economy. There are many thousands of people who have been laid off from their jobs. These people may be interested in your opportunity. However, if you approach them with your opportunity as soon as you hear of their misfortune, you risk being perceived as an "ambulance chaser," which will forever ruin your chances of them taking an open minded look at your business.

If you approach them from the standpoint of "now what are you going to do?" they will reject any offer you give them. It is better that they "discover" what you have as an opportunity for them to regain their dignity. You want them to understand that your business opportunity can and will help them in their time of need, but often you will only reach them if you allow them to "stumble" upon the idea themselves.

You enable them to "stumble" upon your opportunity by first having a genuine conversation with them, and about them. You must not make the conversation about you and your "great opportunity" that can "save the day." You must ask the right questions to allow them to talk about their situation.

Asking a person questions without broadcasting your motives is often more difficult than you might think. Once they feel you are genuinely interested in them and their situation, they will become open to ideas and suggestions. This process may take several conversations before they are ready to hear about what you have to offer.

The other reality is that they may never be ready. That's okay because you have gained a friend in the process by being a good listener. Sometimes a good friend can be more valuable to your business than a business partner.

> Sometimes a good friend can be more valuable to your business than a business partner.

Honesty is the key. If after listening to their needs and speaking with them about your business, you discern that what you have to offer is not best for them, say so. They will appreciate your honesty. If you just try to "get them into your business" at all costs, it will cost you in the long run. Not only will you start a reputation of insincerity, but they will never recommend anyone else to your business. This one mistake could potentially cost you thousands of dollars in lost income.

Another type of person looking for extra income is the person who is trying to hedge against his investment losses. This is currently a wide spread problem in our economy. Because of the decline in our economy over the past few years, people whose retirement savings are tied to the stock markets have experienced a sharp decline in the value of their savings.

These individuals are looking for ways to fill in the gaps produced by these losses. They are also afraid that when the time comes, there will not be enough left in those accounts to survive their retirement years. They are willing to work extra hours now in order to make up the difference for those losses, which provides an excellent opportunity for you to gain momentum in your network marketing business.

How you approach this group of people is just as important as it was for the last group. The majority of these people are more affluent, and therefore, more business savvy. They already understand the value of their efforts. This type of person is not looking for another job, but is willing to take on extra work, as long as the reward is in line with their goals.

This group is much more discriminating when it comes to the type of business with which they are willing to work. Of course, you should always be professional in your approach, but this group generally responds more to professionalism. The people in this group are often more willing to spend money when it is necessary in order to make money. They may already understand the value of leverage.

These people tend to be more aware that what they are doing now affects their future. They have been planning for retirement for many years, and they are looking forward to when they can actually say goodbye to their job. Since their retirement portfolio lost value, they need extra income to ensure their ability to retire when they had originally planned.

This group of people usually has a large circle of friends with whom they have a measure of influence already. It is this circle of friends that is their "warm market" when they enter into business with you. You would do well to help them cultivate this circle in the right way. You do not want them to "go after" their friends without first having the proper training, which would result in their warm market turning cold.

This group is often the largest demographic in many organizations. This is because the motivation found in this group is usually much greater than in other people. Most of the time, this group is also in the middle age range. They are more established in the community and have less time to prepare for retirement than a younger generation. This motivation is contagious which produces a very high level of excitement.

People that simply desire to have more freedom in their life are typically business owners. They may already have a small business. They are in business for themselves because they enjoy the freedom having their business brings them. These people may be looking for additional income because their business is suffering due to the Moose economy. They realize if things get worse in the economy, they may potentially lose their business. This is a reality for many business owners. The economy is not the only reason businesses have closed here in the United States.

The North American Free Trade Agreement (NAFTA) is also an influence on businesses that has been instrumental in many businesses here in the USA closing their doors. It does not matter whether you agree or disagree about the political aspects of NAFTA, the fact still remains that it caused many businesses here in the United States to go under.

When you approach someone with your opportunity who is self employed, it is wise to first know a little about them and their business. As with anyone else, you must show a genuine interest in them. When you are informed about their business, chances are, you will be perceived as genuine and will more readily relate to them. In this way, they know you are not just concerned with yourself, but are interested in their livelihood as well. This also helps them to perceive you as someone who is in tune with the business world.

Business owners who are looking for more freedom in their lives are more likely to understand the importance of the opportunity you have to offer them. They are more apt to see the benefits of owning a part-time business because they are already a business owner.

Those who have financial goals and are looking for ways to reach those goals are very goal-oriented in almost every area of their life. Their financial goals are just one area to which they are strongly connected. Once you understand a person's motivations, their actions are perfectly logical. For the person who is goal-oriented, you must present your opportunity in logical steps, broken down into attainable tasks.

For goal-oriented people, there is a sense of security in the whole process, not just in reaching the particular goal. Many times, this person will simply replace a goal they have met with one that is not yet reached. Once you have determined a goal-oriented person to be a prospect, you can approach them from the standpoint of unfinished tasks they may have in their financial goals. These goals could include leaving a financial heritage and helping family members.

Regardless of the type of person you are dealing with, it is important to be genuine. If you really care about helping people, it will not be difficult to be yourself and, at the same time transparent. Not only are there different types of people searching for additional income, there are also different areas in which they are searching. These include the internet, friends and family, and traditional media.

## Internet

People are looking for someone or something that will guide them through the maze of available income solutions. Today's searcher is more knowledgeable and skeptical than in the past. The wise entrepreneur will learn where these searchers are looking, what they are looking for, and how to deliver the right message and information to them. This is the open secret of marketing.

The savvy entrepreneur knows the internet is the platform for the "media empires" of the future. The internet has changed how marketing strategies are employed. If you want to do well in your business, you will learn all you can about the use of the internet as a marketing tool.

## Friends and Family

Word of mouth advertising is still the ultimate form of spreading the word about something. This is the oldest of all marketing techniques. Before television, radio, or even the printed (or chiseled) word, word of mouth was the most effective way of communicating. When a person wanted to gather information, they asked someone who they thought might have the answer. This still happens today, just in different ways.

There is no better way to gain credibility than for someone who knows you to tell someone they know that you are the expert. The important thing is that, when this happens, you really must be the expert. If you deliver, chances are there is a massive following of people that awaits you. The ability to quickly reach masses of people through word of mouth is perhaps the most prestigious of all the marketing methods. This phenomenon is called viral marketing.

## *Traditional Media*

Many "so-called" network marketing gurus are telling people that old network marketing strategies are no longer useful. Anyone who tells you traditional marketing techniques do not work is probably trying to sell you something. And it is probably their "system" which, of course, is light years ahead of everyone else's. Beware of these people!

The old standard of holding meetings and talking to people one-on-one is still a very viable way to market your business. While some of these techniques are not truly leveraging your time, they are still necessary. Never pass up the opportunity to utilize anything that will help you grow your business.

Old marketing techniques are bad only if they are unethical, illegal, do not work, or cause harm in some way. Then again, this goes for the new marketing techniques as well. Loosen up the reins a little. Enjoy what you are doing. Going to meetings and having the chance to influence someone in a positive way can be fun.

You can use the newspaper, radio, television, direct mailings, and personal invitations to run an advertising campaign about your business meetings or even your opportunity. In today's economy, people are looking for anything they can find to make an additional income. Use this to your advantage. You must simply remember to use caution when advertising, so as not to cross any company policy or procedural issues. You do not want to get into a legal battle over a mistake in an advertisement.

It is always best to consult your company policies before you advertise in a public forum. Most companies have written guidelines you can follow, but it may be more prudent to actually talk to a person who can advise you on the course of action you may need to take. This is not said to deter you from advertising, but to advise you to use wisdom and caution.

Traditional media is still a very productive means of marketing your business. You have to look for the opportunities that best suit your business and personality. Not every form of traditional media will always work for you. It is up to you to decide which ones will or will not.

Traditional marketing has a place in your collection of marketing strategies. Do not "throw the baby out with the bath water." A person who uses both traditional and modern marketing methods will be much more successful in the long run.

## *Apprentice and Authority*

No one jumps into network marketing as an expert; everyone starts out as an apprentice. An apprentice is anyone who is either searching for answers or who just became a representative of the network marketing company of his choice. There are several levels of skill and ability that you can move up to from the apprentice level; I call this the "Marketing Competency Scale." It is as follows:

1. Apprentice

2. Intermediate

3. Proficient

4. Expert

You must identify where you are on this scale. This will help you determine if you have any weaknesses and how to address them. Each section of the scale has a graduated skill set. You will find that you may have already mastered some skills in the category you are currently in.

One of the biggest problems in network marketing is that most representatives are taught very few skills, and, for the majority, personal development is an area that is lacking. This segment is designed to help you identify your strengths and weaknesses and to build your weaknesses to make them strengths. Although you may have mastered all but one or two points in a level, and have already moved to the next stage, do your best to master all abilities on every level.

### *Apprentice:*

An apprentice is anyone who is new to network marketing or to a particular network marketing company. Because an apprentice has just started his business, it is possible that he has little or no experience in network marketing. There are those who have prior involvement in network marketing who are very knowledgeable about the industry and even the company they were previously associated with, but they would still fall into the apprentice category because they still need to be educated about their new company.

The apprentice generally has no knowledge of marketing strategies and has only begun to grow his business. Most of the time, the representative in this stage is at least familiar with the compensation plan and company policies. Therefore, he may have a few representatives in his downline because he is able to convey his opportunity, but is unable to answer some questions.

It is at this stage that we find representatives with the most zeal and fervor for their business. The excitement level and attitude of the apprentice is very positive and uplifting. This is why it is very important that new representatives attend weekly business presentation meetings, because it is encouraging to the more seasoned representatives as well as prospective distributors.

### An apprentice:

1. Has identified that he wants to do and have more.

2. Searches for the best opportunity to suit his needs.

3. Can identify what network marketing business he will join.

4. Joins the business of his choice.

5. Learns how to share his business with others.

6. Makes himself familiar with company policies and the compensation plan.

7. Learns how to enroll others into his business.

8. Learns about the company's products and services.

9. Has a positive attitude and a willingness to learn.

10. If available, attends local weekly business presentations.

This is a vital time in the life of your business. Though it is in the apprentice stage that most network marketers fail, those who continue on and learn enough to take the next step increase their chances of success.

### *Intermediate:*

The representative who falls into the intermediate category is actively working to grow his business. He graduates from the apprentice stage by adding a few customers and representatives to his business. This gives the intermediate distributor confidence and confirms his decision to choose this industry and company.

Though the intermediate has some prior experience, he is still learning the basics of his business. He is beginning to grasp the concept of where to find prospective representatives. He learns that though someone may not be interested in becoming a representative, they may still be interested in purchasing a product or service from him, so he leaves no stone unturned.

The intermediate representative knows the policies, the procedures, and the compensation plan and is able with some dexterity to explain it to others. He is attending weekly meetings and is actively involved in them. Some who are in the intermediate stage are comfortable with introducing the speaker or giving announcements while others simply greet visitors and make others feel welcome.

### *An Intermediate:*

1. Has started his business and actively works to see it grow.

2. Is beginning to grasp the basics.

3. Is learning what to look for in a prospective representative.

4. Does not give up when someone says no.

5. Is active at the local business presentation meetings.

6. Knows the policies and procedures and compensation plan.

7. Is watching the leaders and emulating them.

8. Is a student of his business.

9. Is coachable/teachable.

10. Is learning different marketing strategies.

The intermediate knows little of marketing techniques and is still a follower. He sees the leaders of the company and wants to become one, but has much to learn before he gets to that point. This too is a dangerous time in the life of his business because he may have zeal and enthusiasm which, when coupled with a lack of understanding, can be offensive to potential customers and representatives. If this uneducated passion is taken in the wrong way by prospects, it can produce negative results.

## Proficient:

The representative who has graduated from intermediate to proficient did so by building an organization that is now growing, not because of his direct efforts, but because of his leadership. He has come to understand that there is more to network marketing than traditional marketing practices, and he is continually endeavoring to better himself through personal development and leadership roles.

The proficient representative is comfortable giving a presentation in front of a crowd. This person gives the business presentation enough to know it inside and out. He understands the compensation plan, the policies, the procedures, and the company's products and services well enough to clearly explain them to others.

This representative has learned the basics and is very knowledgeable in traditional business practices. He has a good marketing knowledge and is honing his marketing skills. When he reaches this stage, he understands not only what he is doing, but why he is doing it and why what he is doing works.

Generally, the proficient representative has built what most would consider a medium sized organization and is seeing regular growth in his business. He has begun coaching and instructing the representatives in his downline. He also takes responsibility for the outcome of his business. Because his level of understanding has grown, his confidence has grown with it. He now speaks with authority and is learning to become the leader.

### A Proficient:

1. Is able to give the regular business presentation comfortably.

2. Understands and is able to clearly explain the compensation plan, policies and procedures, and products and services.

3. Has a basic knowledge of traditional business practices.

4. Understands there is more to marketing than traditional strategies.

5. Has become adept at marketing his business.

6. Is coaching those in his downline.

7. Has a medium sized organization.

8. Takes responsibility for his actions.

9. Exudes a strong level of confidence.

10. Is learning to become the leader.

Though this may be a good position, if this is the final goal of a representative he will arrive here and stagnate in his business. There is still one more level the network marketer should strive to achieve. If the proficient representative continues being coachable and teachable, he has a good chance of becoming an expert.

### Expert:

The expert graduates from the proficient level by continuing to grow not only his business, but himself. When a representative reaches the level of expert, the dynamics of his business have clearly changed. By no means does this mean he has "arrived."

The expert has a relatively large organization which has taken a life of its own and will now grow with less proactive interaction. He has a great deal of experience and is proficient in both traditional and contemporary business practices and marketing strategies. He has the knowledge and is apt to teach the policies and procedures, compensation plan, and the company's products and services to others.

This person has confidence to do persuasive presentations consistently and can teach presentation techniques and marketing strategies to those in his downline. He understands that when he sponsors a new representative they are not joining his business; they are joining him.

The expert is the authority in his network marketing business. Others look to the authority for answers and guidance. Part of being the expert and the authority is being a leader. To be an effective leader he must understand not only the business, but how people think and respond to certain challenges.

As the leader, the expert is very confident and is not affected by the criticisms or praises of others. He has learned how to focus on accomplishing the goals he set for himself and is very intent in his actions. He does not allow circumstances or people to sway him and is always positive and uplifting to those around him.

He offers value to those who follow him. He respects the time and personal space of others, treating them with integrity, and demands the same for himself. He dresses with style and takes care of his body by living a healthy lifestyle and encourages others to do the same.

*An Expert:*

1.  Has much experience.

2.  Is skillful in traditional and contemporary business practices and marketing strategies.

3.  Teaches others the compensation plan, policies and procedures, and specifics of the products and services of the company.

4.  Is very confident in his actions.

5.  Can give persuasive business presentations consistently.

6.  Has a deeper understanding of people and his business.

7.  Has a relatively large organization.

8.  Is viewed as valuable by others.

9.  Respects others and demands the same for himself.

10. Is always positive.

As the leader, the expert must be the authority. Authority is influence that creates respect and confidence; this influence is established when three things are recognized in the expert.

1.  Competence - He is the source of instruction, correct information and wise advice.

2.  Confidence - He is confident in his knowledge and ability to motivate others as well as himself.

3.  Control - He is not only in control of himself, but of his future as well.

Personal development and leadership are both an ongoing task. As stated previously, no one jumps into this business as an expert; everyone starts out as an apprentice. Therefore, an apprentice must start somewhere. He must learn from someone, recognize the authority, and build his skills.

The quicker he recognizes and begins to learn from the authority, the sooner he can become the authority himself. Some will grow and move up the competency scale faster than others. Even the apprentice can see measures of success and must sometimes position himself as the authority.

The appearance of being an authority on a subject can be a byproduct of leadership. People will naturally follow a leader. But, just because a person is the authority on something does not make him a good leader. This is why it is vital to build and enhance personal development and leadership skills. No matter what level you find yourself in network marketing, you must position yourself as the authority. You can do this in several ways.

1.  Teach others – In teaching others you become valuable. People are searching for answers. When you become the source of information you position yourself as the authority.

2.  Be a pioneer in your business – A pioneer blazes a trail for others to follow. When you can make it easier for others you will be viewed as the authority.

3.  Provide good content – Content is the manifestation of intent. This manifestation must be powerful. Authority is recognized by gaining acknowledgement from other people who read the content.

There is a difference between content and information. Someone who provides information is not always the authority since information is simply random facts and statistics. Content is information that leads the reader to a conclusion and calls them to action. The quality of the content is what distinguishes the authority and exposes the novice.

The quality of the content must meet what I call "The Four Requirements of Power and Value" in order for the intent to be accomplished. The four points of the "Power and Value Guide" are as follows:

1. Be relevant to their current circumstances.

2. Provide answers to their questions.

3. Connect with them on an emotional level.

4. Identify with their past experiences.

Becoming an authority produces the platform which enables you to reveal, offer, or withhold opportunities from others. The apprentice must go to the authority for information, instruction, wisdom, and advice. The money is made by the leader when the masses begin to follow. Who do you want to be–the authority or the apprentice? People are searching; you must position yourself in a place where people are looking so they find you and come to you for a solution.

## Being Coached and Coaching

### The Coach

Arthur L. Williams, founder of A.L. Williams & Associates (known also as Primerica Financial Services), said, "No one wants a boss; everyone loves a coach." The idea that bosses are just a thorn in the employee's side is a common misconception purveyed among workers. Still, many believe bosses were only created to make forty hours of every week as miserable as possible. But when you speak to someone about their coach, you can see they have fond memories of the days when they were under the guidance of their coach.

The interesting thing is that the coach caused a great deal of pain and grief through conditioning exercises and early practices, yet the coach is still respected and adored. The boss on the other hand may cause grief and inconvenience and is hated for his drive and demands. The difference is that bosses are perceived to work only for the benefit of the company, while coaches are viewed as working for the team.

A coach is not only the authority on the subject at hand, but is willing and able to train the members of the team. A coach has impact on the lives of the team members by being supportive and by encouraging those working with him. A coach can recognize the strengths and weaknesses of others and build on the strengths.

The coach is the one who prepares the team for the game. He makes himself available to the team and gives instruction, positive feedback, and correction without causing resentment. He provides the resources necessary for team members to sharpen their skills and abilities. The coach values differences in team members and brings them together to form a winning combination.

A good coach does not make decisions based on emotions. He realizes that accurate information and insight are the best guides for the best decisions. A good coach helps the team to grow and strive to be their best. Former Notre Dame Coach Ara Parasheghian said, "A good coach will make his players see what they can be rather than what they are."

## *The Coached*

It is the responsibility of those being coached to respond to the coach by having heart and doing their best. Unfortunately, many today are too selfish to work as team players and participate in a group effort. Henry Ford had a good point when he said, "You will find men who want to be carried on the shoulders of others, who think that the world owes them a living. They do not seem to see that we must all lift together and pull together." When team members work together, they have a competitive edge and a much better chance of winning.

Apply this to your local weekly business presentation meetings. If everyone on the team (in the organization) were to be faithful to the meetings and participate by speaking to others and doing their best to bring others to the meeting, it would change the dynamics of the meeting. People would see that something is happening, and the perception of the visitors would be to get in on this before it is too late.

It is imperative that the person who is being coached be teachable. He should have a willingness and desire to learn. Pride often prevents people from being coached because they are unwilling to submit to the coach. The coach is not always the oldest person in the room; you must recognize the authority of the coach, submit to that authority and defer to the coach's expertise.

## Coaching

The goal of coaching in your network marketing business is to produce a team of well educated representatives who are capable not only of succeeding but also of helping others succeed. Coaching is a partnership between the trainer and the trainee, and each party must be willing to give of themselves in order to see positive results.

There are four levels of competency, and each of the four levels can train any level below them. The apprentice can coach others by helping them realize their need for what he has. The intermediate can coach the apprentice, the proficient the intermediate, and so on.

If you are going to coach someone in your network marketing business you can use these four steps to coaching. I have developed an acrostic to help you remember it with the word I.D.E.A.

1.  Identify – Discover their strengths.

2.  Develop – Cultivate those strengths into skills specific to network marketing.

3.  Execute – Implement those skills with a solid business model.

4.  Apply – Promote that business model with proper marketing strategies.

There are a number of coaching tools available today and equally as many techniques. You must discover your technique and the way that works best for you when it comes to coaching and training others. You must be the leader and leaders must win the hearts of their followers.

Motivational speaker Bob Nelson said, "You get the best effort from others, not by lighting a fire beneath them, but by building a fire within." As a coach you want to provide motivation and inspiration to those around you. One of the keys of motivation is getting people to believe that they have within themselves what it takes to get the job done.

When attempting to motivate people, remember what college football coach Homer Rice said: "You can motivate by fear, and you can motivate by reward, but both of those methods are only temporary. The only lasting thing is self motivation."

In network marketing, it is not about you. It is about the team. It is about learning to coach those in your organization and teaching them to coach others as well. Help them find that drive and inspiration from within and your team will go much farther.

# chapter 19

## the action guide

*"why walk when you can fly!"*

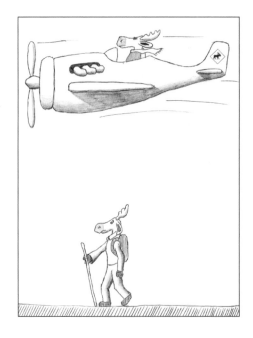

## chapter 19

# the action guide

*"why walk when you can fly!"*

You live in St. Louis, MO and decide to take a trip to the Oregon Coast for an extended vacation. You have always wanted to follow the Oregon Trail, and this is your chance. As you speak with family and friends about your plans, someone suggests that you walk the whole way to relive the experience of the early pioneers.

What a great idea! You have a very pioneering spirit; why not a pioneering adventure to go with it? You determine you cannot leave without first making preparations, so you spend four months getting into shape and walking to prepare for your vacation. Soon your vacation time arrives and you begin walking down the street at a steady pace.

Things are going very well. You are enjoying the scenery, taking in all the sights and sounds. You meet many good people along the way, and before you know it, you feel great about your progress. You have had your shoes for several months so they are broken in and comfortable yet still in good enough shape to carry you to the coast.

As you walk along, you realize the benefits of your mode of travel. The fresh air and the exercise are so good for your health; besides that, you really enjoy it. Other people use their cars, but you are content with walking. Pretty soon you cover a few more miles and you begin to think, "This is great, I am actually getting somewhere."

Everything seems to be going very well until, after several days of walking, you realize, it is a long way to Oregon! When you started on this journey you did not think about how far away Oregon actually was. You begin to believe you have made a mistake by choosing to walk.

> Americans have been taught to get a good education and find a good job working for someone else, and therefore choose an inadequate vehicle to carry them to retirement.

You needed a much faster vehicle to get you to such a distant destination. Now you will spend all your vacation time walking, leaving you no time to enjoy the coast. This is not what you envisioned when you began your journey. You thought you could have the best of both worlds by enjoying the journey and the destination. Consequently, all your time was taken up walking. Had you made the trip faster, you would have much more time to enjoy the vacation. (Good idea gone bad!)

Now you feel trapped. You have already been walking for days, entrusting the success of your extended vacation to this now inadequate mode of transportation. The journey is too long for walking in such a short period of time. You cannot go back now, after having gone so far. What are you going to do? How can you change vehicles after all this time? You were so comfortable and even excited about walking. Is there something you can do to make this journey faster so you at least have some time to spend on the Oregon Coast?

Many people find themselves in this same situation. In this allegory, the preparation represents college; the journey, life; the shoes, a job; and the vacation, retirement. Unfortunately, all too often this allegory is a reality. Americans have been taught to get a good education and find a good job working for someone else, and therefore choose an inadequate vehicle to carry them to retirement.

They believe they are going to fulfill their dreams by working for someone else, which is rarely the case. As an employee, you may make a good salary and have many benefits, but you certainly do not have true freedom. Even with an IRA, 401K, or any other retirement savings account, the economy is too unpredictable for a dependable retirement income.

Recently I was talking with a man who has been working for the same company for almost thirty years. He told me his retirement account has all but evaporated, and is now diminished to the level it was twelve years ago. He believes he will lose a lot more before the economy turns around or he retires. Working for other people is not the answer to financial freedom. Nothing is guaranteed, especially when so heavily influenced by outside forces.

The best guarantee you can have is to take charge of your life and gain control of your finances. The financial vehicle you choose for this task makes all the difference in the outcome. Just as in the story, when a person chooses to work for someone else, he is hinging his financial outcome on a job and ultimately on his employer. If there is a better way, why walk when you can fly?

Many people are finding that having a home-based business is both personally fulfilling and financially rewarding. The choice to take charge of your life is sometimes intimidating. Because many people are accustomed to being told what to do, they do not know what to do once they are given the opportunity to be in control of their life. This is one of the barriers preventing people from owning a business.

> Working for other people is not the answer to financial freedom.

"Breaking away from the herd" of being an employee may be just the stimulus you need to begin your journey to financial freedom. You do not have to stop walking right away or ever stop walking, if that is what you want. Becoming a network marketer does not require you to quit your current job.

Taking charge of your financial future is accomplished through first educating yourself in opportunities that produce a part-time income. This does not mean you do it in your "free time." This means you do it "part-time." There is a huge difference. To do something "part-time" means you set aside a pre-determined number of hours each week to work on that endeavor, while for most people "free time" is hard to find.

There is a progression in the mind and actions of the network marketing business owner. What begins as a desire blossoms into a business. This development does not happen by accident, but by design. All too often, it is this design that remains a mystery to all but those who are seen as successful.

You have already learned that in order to succeed, you must have a plan, work your plan, prepare and grow yourself through personal development, and use the best tools for the job. You understand as a business owner, it is important for you to become a leader. Leadership is useless without people, because people are the driving force of any business. This information, thorough as it may be, can still be useless without an Action Guide.

A daughter of General William Booth once said, "To change your future, you must disturb the present," The Action Guide does not determine the outcome of your business, but rather helps you discover what direction your business should go. This Action Guide will take you by the hand and reveal to you the next step you need to take.

This chapter is dedicated to defining the step-by-step process that network marketers must take in order to see greater measures of success in their business. This guide is a duplicable process that you internalize and adapt to your particular needs. You will use this as the foundation for your business model. This process is relevant and necessary to the business of each individual and should be taught to others to promote their success as well.

I recently went to a seminar where the speaker was talking about financial success. He mentioned in passing his idea of three keys to success. They were knowledge, opportunity, and action. When I thought about the three simple words he used, I began to think about them and have expounded on them here for you.

Gaining knowledge, having the right opportunity, and taking the appropriate action are three fundamentals of success. Each element is very important, but without the other two it will not build the right foundation for success. Knowledge and opportunity, without action, is like starting a car and putting it into drive while the wheels are suspended in the air.

If you have knowledge and opportunity but do not take action, some would call it a waste, whereas if you seize an opportunity and take action without knowledge, the result can be quite devastating. Realizing the necessity of all three, you might ask why someone would ignore any one of the three keys, yet it happens every day.

The application of knowledge, opportunity, and action is significant in every stage of life. This process is the only way you can move from one step to the next. You must gain the right knowledge, find the best opportunity, and take the appropriate action.

Prior to this chapter, you have been given the first of the three keys. There is now a "door of opportunity" open to you; an opportunity to discover your path to success. Your action upon this opportunity will determine the level of success you will experience. As some would say, this is "where the rubber meets the road," and "what separates the men from the boys."

## Desire

The establishment of every business is rooted in desire. Whether it is the desire of one person or a group of people, that desire is fundamental to the drive of the business owner(s). Napoleon Hill said, "Desire is the starting point of all achievement; not hope, not a wish, but a keen pulsating desire which transcends everything." Desire is the longing or craving for something more; it comes from being unsatisfied or lacking contentment in your current state or position.

Desire is often a result of a combination of things. Sometimes a desire may be produced by seeing what someone else has, and wanting the same for yourself. It can also come from learning about something new which creates the knowledge of different possibilities. People who have the desire for more are often advised to become acquainted with those who have and do more. This is because we as human beings are influenced by our surroundings and our peers. When your desires change, the company you keep, your habits, and your surroundings will often reflect that change.

You will find that your desires will cause you to dream when you allow your mind to shape an image of what you want. When you see what you want in your mind's eye, you can begin to visualize ways to make that dream a reality. Napoleon Hill may have said it best when he said, "Whatever the mind can conceive and believe the mind can achieve."

You must make the distinction between your dreams and your desires. Desires are the foundation of your dreams. Your dream of someday going on vacation to some exotic place and having no fear or anxiety about your finances is a result of you first having the desire to become financially free. Dreams are the pictures that desire will paint on the canvas of your imagination.

> "Whatever the mind can conceive and believe the mind can achieve."

Your desires will call you to action. It is only through action that you will begin to make your dreams and wishes a reality. Without action, desire will only remain a dream. For most people, desire will cause them to begin searching. What is found as a result of that search has much to do with the life of that desire. If, in your search, you were to find that there was a great opportunity available to you, your desire would more than likely grow and you would continue to act upon your knowledge. If your search were to prove fruitless, chances are that desire would stagnate and your energy would be redirected.

A desire is often embodied in hope. A wise proverb says, "Hope deferred maketh the heart sick: but when the desire cometh, it is a tree of life." Hope is the expectation that your desires will come to pass, and, when you do not see your desire come to pass as quickly as you think it should, you may find yourself losing hope and giving up.

It was stated earlier that the establishment of every business is rooted in desire. The same holds true for the continued life of your network marketing business. Businesses will sometimes change with the times, but at the foundation of that business remains desire.

There are several factors that may have an effect on someone's desire. As a business owner gains knowledge and experience, he may see new opportunities arise that were not previously available. People get tired of doing the same thing all the time and occasionally want a change of scenery. When goals are accomplished and dreams are realized, horizons are broadened and new desires emerge.

Sometimes the redirection of desire is a result of something as simple as a change in life, people move, have children, become grandparents, get promotions, change jobs, or get tired of the daily grind. Life changes have produced desires, and those desires have produced obvious transformations in some people's businesses.

As a business grows, the desire of the owner may change. For instance, at the birth of a new business, the owner wants to nurture and grow his new business to prove that it can survive. Later, his desire may change to refining the products and services or to becoming known as the company with the best customer service in town.

The same holds true for your network marketing business. When you begin you may simply have a desire to get your business started and make a little extra money each month. While you continue to grow your business, you may see your desires change which may shift your focus to taking your business to a higher level, helping others grow their business, or growing your business to a point where you can go full time or even retire early.

You already understand that in every stage of life you must have knowledge, opportunity, and action. Therefore, it is safe to say that you understand the importance of acting upon your desires. Learn about every aspect of your desire. Search for the opportunity that will bring your desire to pass. Often in your quest for knowledge, the opportunity will reveal itself. Gain the knowledge, find the opportunity, and then act on it. As A.L. Williams said, and Nike chanted for years, "Just Do It!"

## Information and Knowledge

The dentist in our opening story stood frozen for a brief second after the moose fell so close to where he stood. I like to imagine he had several things that ran through his mind in that brief instant.

Perhaps his life passed before his eyes as he reflected on the moose turning and charging at him in a rage. He might have thought of his dentistry practice, or about the new pool they planned to have installed next spring. While the moose was charging, had he understood the gravity of the situation, he would have thought more about how he would survive that moment.

Whatever his thoughts were, one thing is for certain, if he had known more about the temperament of a moose beforehand, he would not have placed himself in such a predicament. But it was too late for that once he fired his first shot. In the few seconds after that shot, all the knowledge of his firearm and the moose itself would merge into one critical action. Even though it took four more shots to finally kill the raging beast, it was his persistence to keep shooting that finally stopped it.

It is the use of information that makes it important. If the dentist had known to wait for the best shot in the first place, the outcome of the story would have been much different. There are four main reasons why information is important, and they are all interrelated. The four main reasons are:

1. It is necessary for knowledge.

2. It is the catalyst for creativity.

3. It possesses the potential for inspiration.

4. It can create desire when coupled with inspiration.

It is often said that knowledge is power, and it certainly is, but are knowledge and information the same things? Think of how many people would love to know when a certain stock was going to move up dramatically. Someone could make a lot of money with that kind of information.

I spent eight years in the Army Signal Corps, with the 81st and 120th ARCOM. My military occupational specialty was in satellite communications. Electronic communications are the preferred method for the transfer of information. They play such an important role in battlefield decisions because speed and accuracy are essential to the delivery of vital information for making correct tactical decisions. The question is, when does information become knowledge?

Does the information about the stock mean anything if it is not used at the right time? Is the battlefield information valuable if it does not make sense to the commander and is not used to make correct decisions? The answer to both of these is, of course, no. Information is only random data that has no significance until it is organized into a meaningful structure. This structure generates organized thoughts, which are then used to create ideas that can produce powerful and valuable content. It is this content, coupled with desire, which moves people to action.

Information can only become knowledge when it is specific to a person's need, organized into meaningful categories, accessible to the right people, and relevant enough to have purpose. These are the four attributes that make information valuable. They can be easily remembered as the acrostic S.O.A.R.

Specific
Organized
Accessible
Relevant

## Specific

Information that is specific allows a person to make appropriate decisions. If information is not specific, there are too many questions that must be answered before appropriate action can be taken. You need specific information to successfully run your network marketing business, such as how you are compensated, to whom you are marketing, and what products or services are available through your company. These questions are specific, and you will need specific information regarding them.

## Organized

When information is organized it becomes recognizable to the individual. This recognition occurs because of the relevance of the information to the need of the individual. This information can then be organized further by the individual to be used in various ways. The information then becomes valuable to he who chooses to use it. This value is then demonstrated by the manner in which the information is used.

In network marketing, information seems to be in endless supply. There are as many "systems" or "secrets" as there are companies. Everyone wants an edge in growing their business. There is nothing wrong with wanting to grow your business. The problem is that there are some who prey on unsuspecting distributors by selling them a "cutting edge top secret system" that "the top network marketers do not want you to know about." Many of these "systems" are nothing but a network marketing company in themselves, some of which are not much more than a scheme.

There is nothing wrong with producing a system that truly helps people grow their business, as long as it is legitimate, and it does not conflict with the company's policies. There are few places where you can go to receive information that does not cost an enormous amount of money. There are only a few legitimate systems or secrets that truly help people grow their business.

Anyone can do research on network marketing, selling, marketing, and a number of other topics related to this industry to produce a body of knowledge that helps them do better in their business. There is a wealth of information available that will help a person understand what this industry is all about, and tips on how to be successful in it. The information that makes sense can be used to help grow your business. Some information may not make sense, but should not be dismissed because there is a chance it is only misunderstood. As a person learns more about the network marketing industry, they may use this information at a later date.

### Accessible

I went to my friend Patrick's house a few months ago to give him a hand with his broken washing machine. Being an aviation mechanic, he has a reasonable sense of mechanical skills. When I arrived he had the machine already disassembled and had located the problem. A little plastic piece responsible for turning the drum of the washer had broken. This was a simple fix. Just pop the old broken piece off and push a new one on.

It was Saturday and most repair shops were closed. We called around and found a repair man who was "on call." He said he was in the area that day, had the part, and could even deliver (for a price, of course). Patrick began speaking with him and asked him if he had any advice on the best way to repair it, to which the repair man replied, "I can't tell you that over the phone, it's my little secret."

Disgusted with his unwillingness to help, Patrick finished the phone call and immediately continued calling around to see if he could find anyone else who had the part we needed and could freely offer any advice. He eventually found someone who had the part in stock. As it turned out, the part was cheaper, and the owner was happy to show us a few techniques to make replacing the part easier and faster. Not only that, but later that afternoon, Patrick in his curiosity searched the internet and found the "top secret" information not only readily available, but free.

The "secret agent repair man" lost business that day because he was unwilling to share information. He believed if he could convince Patrick he was the only one with the information, he would win a sale. Unfortunately for him, he did not realize we live in the information age, and when you provide the information people are looking for, they will gladly do business with you.

Information that is not accessible does no one any good. A computer may hold hundreds of gigabytes of information, but unless that information is made available to the person needing it, there is no benefit in it whatsoever. The same can be said for your network marketing business. You may know everything about your business, but until you share this information, it has no value.

If you are faced with the uncertainty of continuing your network marketing business, determine that you will not give up. Learn the whys, what's, and how's of network marketing and then pass what you learn on to those in your organization. Sharing what you have learned with those in your downline will ultimately result in a much larger and stronger organization for you.

### *Relevant*

Even if information is specific, organized and accessible, it must still be relevant to the needs of the person for it to have value. For example, information about how to repair a washing machine has no value to the person repairing an airplane engine, nor is information about how to run a music studio relevant to a plumbing business.

Network marketers need information that is relevant to their business. This information could include, among other things, time management, budgeting, marketing, personal development. It is necessary for you to convey as much relevant information as possible to your team. This will help them grow as individuals and grow their businesses, and it establishes you as the "go to" person for your group.

Information is also the catalyst for creativity. It is important to understand that information is only the catalyst. Information without knowledge, desire, or inspiration is dry and useless. However, information with inspiration, desire, and knowledge, can help a painter create a masterpiece. It is information, coupled with knowledge that helps heads of state make critical decisions that affect the entire nation.

> Information along with desire can cause a person to change the complete course of their life.

Information and desire also go hand-in-hand. Information along with desire can cause a person to change the complete course of their life. Many times this is the case of a person who gets started in network marketing. They have been working for someone else all their life and realize they will never gain financial freedom this way. They choose to start their business because they desire to have something more than the average employee.

Information becomes knowledge when it is understood, theoretically or practically, through experience and education. You can have information without knowledge, but you cannot have knowledge without information. Knowledge makes information powerful. It guides action, reveals authority, and helps you recognize opportunities. When combined with desire, knowledge creates action.

## Opportunity

Sun Tzu (A Chinese philosopher and military strategist best known for his book, *The Art of War*) said, "Opportunities multiply as they are seized." As you become more established in your business, opportunities for additional income will become more apparent to you. Your skills and knowledge will become a valuable asset which can be monetized through the use of the internet and other outlets. Be patient with this process, and allow it to be cultivated rather than forced. Allow people to "discover" you, rather than trying to convince them you have what they are looking for.

Once you have been established as the authority, opportunities will open to you that you would not otherwise have. As the authority, you will become the leader. You will be called upon for answers and advice. This allows you the opportunity to influence others. This influence is revealed through invitations for coaching and training sessions, both locally and abroad. You may even develop coaching and discovery sessions in your local area.

Most people in network marketing say they have a "great opportunity" to offer. This is a poor way of communicating their intent. What the prospect really hears is, "I have started this business, and I need you to join me so I can make more money." Whether this is admitted or not does not change the reality; those of us already in a network marketing business need others to join us. There is no shame in this, but pouncing on someone before they have the chance to get to know you is a mistake. Network marketing is a relationship business. Building relationships is key to building a successful network marketing business.

Paul Orberson said, "There are only two ways to make money in America today; either you multiply money or you multiply people." Network marketing is about multiplying people. You must realize for yourself that network marketing is one of the most effective and ethical ways available to the common person to earn a living.

You will naturally grow more as a person and in your business when you allow yourself to explore new areas of opportunity as they become available. When you understand that network marketing is a great way to earn a living or raise you standard of living, you will realize the following:

1.  Opportunities never go away, they just move to another person.

2.  Opportunities can be given and accepted.

3.  Opportunities can be withheld or rejected.

4.  Opportunities can be missed or squandered.

6.  Opportunities can be created and stumbled upon.

7.  Opportunities can be hidden from people.

8.  Not everyone has the same opportunity.

9.  There is a cost associated with every opportunity.

Abraham Lincoln said, "Most people only have two real great opportunities in a lifetime." When my wife and I were presented with the opportunity to start our current network marketing business, we recognized it as a great opportunity and had to decide if this was our first or our last. With the global economy in trouble as it is, we came to the conclusion it might just be our last.

This is not a doom and gloom attitude; it is an acknowledgement of our age and financial position. We decided we should take advantage of this opportunity to hedge against a decline in our investment returns and increase our current income. This is the motivator for many people.

Even though owning a network marketing business is a great way to produce income, you do not always want to present your business as an opportunity. Most people associate opportunity with hype. Be careful not to use this word too heavily. A better word or phrase might be, "income solution." A little creativity here will go a long way.

The best way for other people to see and understand your business solution is to see it working in your life. When you gain a measure of success, they will be more likely to be open minded to what you are showing them. It is more important to build a relationship than to get someone signed up.

As you act appropriately, you will begin to build a good reputation. As your reputation is established, you will have more opportunities to share your income solution with others. "Opportunity can be created when preparation meets hard work." It does not matter how great your opportunity or income solution is; without knowledge or preparation, action or hard work, the best opportunity in your lifetime is of little value.

# *Take Action*

The instructions you will receive in this section will remove the mystery from several aspects of marketing and will explain how to put all the right pieces of the network marketing puzzle together into one powerful course of action. I recommend reading this section several times before you move on to the final chapter. Once you have completed the entire book, you will want to refer to this chapter many times when setting up your new business or moving your current business to a higher level.

We have talked about many different elements of marketing in the previous chapter and covered a broad range of subjects in alphabetical order. Putting these subjects to work for you is the next phase of your business, whether you are just starting out or have been in network marketing for several years. You must first understand that while all these concepts and methods work in harmony with one another, you must be careful in your selection of methods because some of the techniques have limitations which predetermine how effectively they work with the others.

## *Believe It or Not*

Regardless of what many people say, network marketing is selling. It is true that the business model of some network marketing companies lean more toward distribution than selling, but there must always be a transfer of goods or services through sales of some kind. Selling is not limited to the product or opportunity; it also includes selling yourself. Because of this, it is important to know some "do's and don'ts" of selling.

Do not make your sales pitch about you and your product first. This is a very common mistake. You must ask questions that help you discover your prospect's needs and desires. If you place your needs and desires ahead of theirs, you will be viewed as self-serving. This turns people off almost immediately. Just because you like or see value in your product or income solution does not mean everyone else does. In fact, very few people actually purchase the same things for identical reasons.

Sell benefits and solutions, not features and function. Most people do not care as much about how something works as much as they do about what is does for them or how it makes them feel. For this reason, you should avoid overemphasizing the bells and whistles of your products and opportunity. Instead, you should explain how they can bring about a solution to a specific need they may have.

After identifying their needs and desires, sell yourself before you try to sell your product or opportunity. Everyone in network marketing believes they have the best products, services, pay plan, and company leadership. For your products or business opportunity to stand out from the rest, you must connect with your prospect on an emotional level. Most of the time, this connection is made after they recognize you are genuine. Trust is built when they realize you are not just trying to make a sale. This trust takes time to develop and should not be rushed.

### Find the Pearls

As you begin your new business, you will share your income solution with your warm market. You will think of the people you know and consider who may be interested in joining you in your business. If you can, learn to pre-qualify, but do not pre-judge anyone. Some of the most successful distributors were at one time overlooked because they appeared to have been the least likely prospects.

The word prospect has three different meanings, all of which apply in network marketing. The first meaning is to explore or search. The purpose of prospecting is to find what you are looking for. Many people are looking for financial relief from the Moose economy. They can find this relief through owning a network marketing business.

The second meaning is anticipation of a future event. This term is used in network marketing in reference to the anticipated lifestyle possible through financial freedom. We say, "The prospect of time freedom, personal freedom, and financial freedom is very likely, if a person follows through with their network marketing business." There are many anticipated events in the life of the person dedicated and committed to their network marketing business.

The third definition of prospect is a candidate for a purpose. This is fairly simple to understand. Some people have made the analogy of looking for the oyster that has the pearl. They keep looking through all the oysters until they find the one with the pearl, which translates to, sharing their opportunity with people until someone joins their business or buys their products.

Prospecting is a search that begins with the people you know, such as family members, business acquaintances, friends, and co-workers, and is expanded through their friends and acquaintances. Through this process, your business will grow and you may never run out of people with whom to do business. There are many people looking for a business that will allow them to keep their current job and still produce a nice supplemental income. Network marketing can provide the solution for which they are searching.

## Who Is Working for Whom

In a legitimate network marketing business, every person is given the same opportunity. Each distributor has the chance to build his business to produce the desired income. The structure of network marketing can be described as an upside down pyramid, because of the support that is made available from those who are in the upline.

Anyone who has a downline is, of course, someone's upline. Every member of the upline that understands the value and importance of their downline will do everything possible to support them, because they have a vested interest in their success. This is not because the upline is building on the backs of those in the downline. It is because the large scale success of the upline pivots on the success of those in the downline. In corporate America, the CEO, President, and Vice President are rarely affected by the firing or quitting of an employee, but when a representative fails or quits those in the upline are directly affected.

It is the duty of the upline to provide support and motivation for those in their downline. That support may come in the form of training on the company's products or services, giving business presentations for a group in the downline, or simply providing an encouraging word to a discouraged representative. New representatives sometimes experience buyer's remorse when they begin to think about the business they just purchased and the possibility that they might not succeed. The upline should be able to discern when this happens and encourage the new representative.

On the other hand, it is the duty of those in the downline to pursue all possible avenues of available training. Though often the upline may provide the training, it is up to the individual to develop the skills necessary to succeed. Each representative should observe his upline, study what works and adopt the techniques that work best with his personality.

> The majority of great leaders are known to have positive attitudes and to always lift others up around them.

As you grow in your business, you should learn to encourage others. There is a lot to be said about positive people. The majority of great leaders are known to have positive attitudes and to always lift others up around them.

If you have a complaint, you should raise the objection to your upline and management team, not your team members. You must guard against negativity when communicating with your downline. Representatives who do not understand this will eventually destroy the morale of those working with them and in turn destroy their business.

Many people will fall into a trap baited by greed. Sometimes, uneducated and uninformed representatives will misrepresent their businesses as a way to get rich quick. It is the responsibility of all network marketers to dispel this kind of thinking by conveying the truth to their downline.

There is no business proven to make everyone involved rich quickly. Network Marketers do get rich, but rarely, if ever, overnight. Most stories you will hear from those who became wealthy in network marketing tell of the long hard road they had to journey to their success. You cannot depend solely on the efforts of your downline to build your income. Each person is going to see different results as they build their business. Some build fast, some slow, and some not at all.

### Presentation Meetings Are Essential

Presentation meetings are one of the most important activities to building a strong network marketing business. Many so-called experts and gurus on the internet criticize this part of network marketing. Many times when someone is very critical about something, it is a result of either their inability to understand it, be successful at it, or they have been offended by it in some way.

Network marketing is a relationship business, and as such requires a high level of tolerance to people's personalities, mannerisms, methods, and faults. Therefore, network marketing is not for the fainthearted. Some of these internet gurus have been fairly successful, but they have limited their true potential by excluding certain activities and methods. You must be open to all available tools for growing your business.

The presentation meeting is the central hub for access to your business in a particular location. How you conduct your meetings will determine how well your influence is distributed throughout your community. Your meetings are a reflection of both your personality and business. The more professional your meetings are conducted, the more professional you and your business will be perceived to be. This means much to the professional community who have in recent years embraced network marketing in great numbers.

The presentation should always be in compliance with your company's policies. The materials and content should be approved by the company with which you are associated. Once you are sure of these two things, let you imagination and creativity go to work for you.

Outside the room and before the meeting, you may have someone manning a table for visitors to sign in and receive a name tag to wear. If you are having a drawing for door prizes, this is a good time and place to give everyone a ticket for the drawing. It is important to have designated people to greet visitors and make them feel welcome.

Before the meeting begins, playing music sets the mood or tone. Playing small video clips of testimonials gets and holds their attention until the meeting begins. You may even create a slide show to play while people are coming into the room to be seated. These activities keep their minds busy and make for a more relaxed atmosphere. Having a table set up in front of the room gives you the opportunity to offer free promotional material and even material for purchase. Having everything in a neat order and arranged properly will draw people's attention to the table.

The presentation should begin with someone introducing himself and giving a very brief testimonial. Once he is finished giving his testimony, he should introduce the person doing the presentation. It is appropriate to give applause when the speaker is introduced and when he is finished with the presentation. This shows appreciation to the speaker and allows for time to transition to the next activity.

> Managing influence is nurturing relationships with the prospect of leveraging their time in the future.

Having a training or coaching session after the meeting is a good idea because you already have a group of people present and it is more convenient for everyone. Following the presentation and prior to the coaching session is a good time to take a break and allow people to stretch their legs, get a drink, and use the restroom.

Before the break is a good time to make announcements and have the drawing for the door prize. During the break you can play more music, promotional video clips, or other material available through your company. Keep the training session short; about a thirty minute maximum is appropriate. The goal is to leave them wanting more.

There is a powerful persuasive energy found in a meeting room filled with hundreds of other people who are looking for answers. Use that energy to your benefit. When you have the opportunity to sit across the table from someone, do it. Personal interaction is what people are craving in this new age of business.

Although there are many benefits to conducting presentation meetings, you should be aware of an issue concerning leverage. When only traditional marketing methods are used, time is not truly leveraged. Many of these activities are managing influence rather than leveraging time.

There are those who believe they are leveraging their time by being faithful to business presentations and showing the business to every individual with whom they can schedule a meeting. You may believe that you are creating leverage by attending meetings, participating in conference calls or even giving the presentations yourself, but you are simply managing your influence.

Everyone has a certain amount of influence that is either increased or decreased by how it is managed. Managing influence is nurturing relationships with the prospect of leveraging their time in the future. Although managing influence is not leveraging time, it is a necessary activity. The problem with managing influence is that there is a very small return on your investment in the short term.

In network marketing, leveraging occurs when a representative benefits from the labor of business partners he recruits into his organization. Benefiting from the efforts of others is not the only application of leverage. The greatest leverage of your time is accomplished by delivering your message to as many people as possible at once. While presenting your business opportunity to one person is necessary, is not fully leveraging your time.

> The greatest leverage of your time is accomplished by delivering your message to as many people as possible at once.

With these thoughts in mind, the presentation meeting is still more than just a presentation of your business opportunity. It is a place of learning for new business owners, a place of encouragement and fellowship with other network marketers, and a place to hone your people skills. Do not ignore this most important asset to your network marketing business.

### Let the People Know You Are There

Trade shows and job fairs are good ways to make your presence known in the community. When deciding where to locate your booth, you may think you are saving money by purchasing a less expensive booth on the back corner, but actually you are not. The difference in pricing between an obscure booth in the back of the room and a corner booth at the entrance or near high-traffic areas should not discourage you from using the better location. In the long run, you will have a much more effective presence in the better location, which will increase your exposure. The more exposure you have, the more likely you are to have better success at recruiting new members and selling your products and services.

Just as with other methods of marketing, when introducing your opportunity, you do not want to come across as being pushy or using hype. They must still see you as the expert or "guru" before they will trust you for their financial future. For this reason, the material you use at these shows and fairs must be informational only and not filled with grand claims.

You should also have an adequate supply of free items to give away. Pens, pencils, wrist bands, name tag lanyards, stress balls, or any other unique item will be very useful in drawing people to your booth. These items are relatively inexpensive and provide not only a draw to your booth but advertisement for your business. Used properly, trade shows and job fairs can provide a list of good leads. It is imperative that you follow up with these leads within a few days of the event. Adding one person to your business is well worth the investment participating in such an event.

### Don't Be Afraid of the Telephone

One of the most dreaded activities of network marketing is that of speaking to someone over the telephone about a business opportunity. Whether that person is a relative, good friend, business acquaintance, or stranger, the fear associated with telling someone about your business can be overwhelming. You may expect me to say something at this point like, "there is really nothing to fear" or, "all you have to do is learn a few good techniques and you'll do fine."

The truth is that many people who have this fear will never get over it. Many people will never call someone about a business opportunity. There are others who dread picking up the phone to make an appointment or sales call, but still do it anyway. I want to help you overcome some of this fear by giving you some insight into human nature and a few techniques that will give you more confidence.

You must identify the root of the fear of telephone marketing. The real fear of telephone marketing is the fear of rejection. This fear is compounded when a person understands they must also possess the skill of verbal persuasion. Most people lack the ability to effectively persuade someone to give up their time to see a business presentation. This is due to poor verbal communication skills and a lack of understanding what motivates people.

Just as a person must learn how to perform well in a profession or trade, you must learn the skills of verbal persuasion. The desire to change your life financially does not come without a price. Part of that price is taking time to develop skills in verbal communications. A biblical proverb says, "A word fitly spoken is like apples of gold in pictures of silver." The meaning of this proverb is just as applicable today as it was thousands of years ago. "Fitly spoken" speaks of words that rise out of conversation naturally and that are easy, not forced or coerced, and therefore are relevant to all the conversation.

These words have power and meaning to all who listen. The visual portrayal of "apples of gold in pictures of silver" is making reference to the pleasing affect on the eye and the obvious pleasant taste to the tongue. In other words, a conversation that is appropriate has all of these qualities and, therefore, makes a lasting impression. Knowing the appropriate thing to say, and saying it at the appropriate time is extremely important. Here are a few tips that can make the task a little easier:

1. Know what you are talking about. Know how your business benefits a wide range of people. Every network marketing business appeals to people differently. Another way of putting it is, any network marketing business appeals in different ways to various types of people. If you know the benefits of your business, you can know how to appeal to a certain kind of person. This requires you to spend time learning about not only your business, but human nature as well. Being knowledgeable about your business will allow you to avoid pitfalls in phone conversations. In other words, you will know what to say and what not to say to the person to whom you are talking.

2. Do not try to sell your opportunity or product over the phone. Most people will not understand what you are trying to tell them anyway. People are visual creatures. They need to see to understand, and the only way they are going to see what you

have to offer is for you to show it to them. The only reason people do not buy your products or services, or join you in your business is because you have not shown them. Most network marketing opportunities are 90% visual. They need to see the benefits of your opportunity. They need to see the compensation plan to understand it. The less you say on the phone, the more money you will make.

3.  Become a professional appointment setter. Instead of trying to explain your business over the phone, you should only make an appointment to show your business. Many people fall into the trap of saying too much while on the phone. Do not confuse the appointment with the presentation. Keep it simple and to the point. You are making an appointment, not trying to convince them to join your business.

    You should get a firm commitment from the person with whom you are making the appointment. You should explain to them up front that you have blocked off a specific amount of time just for them and that you respect their time. Accepting a half-hearted appointment will waste valuable time. If they cannot make a definite appointment for a specific time, do not try and persuade them.

    Timing is important, and now may not be the right time for them. If you are understanding but firm in your resolve to need a definite time, they will respect your time as well, and they will respect you as a person for it. Tell them you will call back next week at a specific time, and follow through with the call. If you fail to follow up with the second call, they will not take you or your opportunity seriously, and you may not get another chance to share your business with them.

4.  Know what you are going to say before you call. Nothing is worse than to make a call and wind

up stuttering and stammering around while they are on the other end of the line, bored out of their mind. You never get a second chance to make a first impression. Knowing what you are going to say up front allows you to practice; therefore, you can get better and better at it. The best way to practice is to make calls. Every situation is different, and with each different situation comes a different opportunity to learn.

What you say and how you initiate the call is of utmost importance. It has been said that most people make a judgment about another person within the first four seconds of a conversation. This is not a lot of time to make a good impression. You must know what you are going to say and why. This first impression will possibly determine how they respond to you from then on. One sure way to make a good impression with someone is to pay them a compliment of some kind.

5.  You should also make sure you have a positive mental attitude before you make a call. When you portray a positive attitude, people will respond to you positively in return. This will ultimately result in a broader influence and stronger business. Having a positive attitude applies to any time you speak to someone about your business, not just over the telephone. No one likes a sourpuss, and if someone sees you with a down-in-the-mouth attitude, they will run from you and your business.

People like to know they are associated with winners. Having a positive attitude tells them you are a winner. Because you are a winner, there should also be an excitement and urgency in your voice when you call. Excitement is contagious, and they will feel your excitement if it is genuine. This excitement comes directly from your attitude.

If you are excited about your business, it is much easier for them to be excited as well.

6. Be specific and brief. The most annoying calls are the ones where the person has everything in the world to say except about the subject at hand. Everyone is busy, and wasting their time is not a good way to make a good first impression. Tell them why you are calling and what you would like them to do. You want them to allow you to take an hour of their time to give them something that will greatly benefit them.

   Make the impression that you are doing them a favor, which you are. Be assertive, but not pushy. End the conversation on a very positive note. You do not need to convince them they have made a good decision to allow you in their home or to come to a meeting. They made the decision themselves, and to say any more would be to insult their intelligence. Recap the place, time, and date of the meeting, thank them for their time and hang up. Continuing to talk at this point will only give them reason to change their mind.

10. How to handle incoming calls about your business: If you utilize the internet and other methods of marketing, you will, without a doubt, receive calls from people who are interested in your business opportunity. How you respond to these calls will make all the difference in how well you connect with the callers. Once they see the opportunity through your marketing efforts and they like what they see, the last part of the equation is your personal connection with them. This is the most critical phase of the relationship because people associate with other people, not with a business opportunity.

    At this stage of the relationship, the caller wants to gain reassurance in their mind that your opportunity is what they want. They also want to clarify any questions they may have, as well as justify logically their emotional decision. I say emotional because, if you delivered powerful wordcopy in your marketing efforts, they connected with you on an emotional level.

What they really want now is to confirm they have made the right decision by justifying it logically. The human element is necessary for their final decision making process. If they are compatible with you, and motivated enough to get started, they will be more open to taking the last step, which is to partner with you in the business.

When you have reached this point, you do not want to overwhelm them or bombard them with more information or pushy tactics. Allow them to discover you and your personality in the time frame in which they are comfortable. After you have built a bond with them and you feel the timing is right, you can use subtle persuasion to move them to the commitment stage by making a suggestion to get started.

If they move forward with the partnership, great, but if they still need more time, respect this and make a suggestion for them to commit to a future follow-up call on a specific date and time. Make the call about them and not about you or your pitch. Use the call as a discovery process. You can very easily find out what their goals are and reasons for looking. Many of their questions will have secondary meanings; learn to recognize these and you will be more successful in the long run.

If you are human, you are eventually going to run out of your warm market. This is one of the reasons for such high attrition in direct sales. Once people exhaust their personal resources, they quit because they do not know what to do next. The advent of the internet developed a venue for reaching more people faster than ever before, creating a nearly infinite source of marketing potential.

## A Website Is a Must

Because network marketing is a relationship business, it is important to have a large circle of people with whom you have a measure of influence. Unfortunately, most of us do not have a very large circle of people we can call upon to share our new-found vehicle to financial freedom. There are a few people in network marketing that actually have this large circle of influence in the beginning stages of their business. This is great for them, but the questions remains "What about everyone else?" Since it is your circle of influence you draw from to build your business, how do you increase your circle?

One way to build your circle of influence is simply to help the people you sponsor to reach their circle of influence, therefore increasing your circle through them. This certainly does work, but the drawback is that it can take a very long time to reach those people in the outer bands of your circle. Because this process can take a long time, many people drop out of the business because they cannot sustain the expenses of their business until their "ship comes in." Their dropping out can result in their "warm market" never being reached.

Most people would love to have an alternative to this warm market. There is such an alternative, and it is found on the internet. With the power of the internet at your fingertips, you can build a massive circle of influence, generated by your website and other marketing tools. There are rules you must follow and techniques you need to implement for the internet to produce a circle of influence large enough to support your business, but once you learn these the sky is the limit to the income you can produce as a result.

The internet and World Wide Web are terms that are many times used synonymously. The fact is that they are not one and the same as many people think. The internet is the hardware components and software platforms necessary to allow the transmission of information via copper wires, fiber optics, and wireless technologies. This information is the heart of the World Wide Web, through the sharing of resources in the form of text documents, images, and videos that are joined by hyperlinks to the available URL's (Uniform Resource Locators).

In the late 1980's, the internet was made available to anyone who had a modem for their computer. The internet quickly became the choice of millions of people for communicating with one another. This shift in social connecting opened the door for businesses to bring advertisements for their goods and services directly into people's homes.

As more businesses started using the internet as their advertising platform, the internet age came to maturity. More and more companies were building websites and making their presence known on the web. This created an internet boom with companies like UUNET, Compuserve, Google, Netscape, Internet Explorer, and many others. These companies offered everything from browsing and file-sharing software to on-line collaboration, emailing, advertising, and chat rooms.

As the internet grew, more stock in these companies was purchased to take advantage of this new phenomenon. In early April 2000, the government declared the Microsoft Corporation to be a monopoly. The anticipation of this news may have contributed to the massive sell off of stocks of most of the larger companies, which took place on Monday morning, March 10. This event is often referred to as the bursting of the "dot com bubble." Due to a lack of understanding of exactly how the World Wide Web would respond to this, many companies went out of business.

> With the power of the internet at your fingertips, you can build a massive circle of influence, generated by your website and other marketing tools.

The bursting of the "dot com" bubble resulted in a shift in the way people viewed the use of the internet and World Wide Web. It is still used for the exchange of information, but in a much more socially interactive way. It is from these events that the term Web 2.0 was created and referred to by the mainstream information technology experts. Web 2.0 is not a tangible item, but rather a concept of the second generation of commerce on the internet.

Wikipedia defines Web 2.0 as, "A perceived second generation of web development and design that facilitates communication, secure information sharing, interoperability, and collaboration on the World Wide Web. Web 2.0 concepts have led to the development and evolution of web-based communities, hosted services, and applications such as social-networking sites, video-sharing sites, wikis, blogs, and folksonomies."

Because of the extraordinary and universal acceptance of the Web 2.0 concept, there has been a surge in social media platforms. These platforms are used as a medium for interaction with not only personal friends and colleagues, but for businesses to gain a following for new product announcements and updates.

Facebook, Ustream, Youtube, Twitter, and many other social media platforms are all considered to be a part of the expanding Web 2.0 concept. Understanding the usefulness of these and other Web 2.0 elements is crucial to deploying a truly effective internet marketing campaign for your network marketing business. Through the implementation of Web 2.0 concepts, we may very well be witnessing the birth of a radical shift in the definition of network marketing altogether.

The term copywriting must not be confused with a copyright. Though copywriting is copyrighted, it is not the act of obtaining the exclusive right to make and sell printed material. Copywriting is one of the more difficult areas of expertise when it comes to internet marketing. You must have great copywriting skills if you are going to reach the right audience with your message. Copywriting is the engine that powers your internet marketing vehicle.

Great copywriting is a skill that can be learned, but you must consider what it will cost in lost revenue during the learning process. Page content must have value to the reader, which is discussed in a previous section with the "Power and Value Guide." If you struggle to connect with people using the printed word, you should probably consider outsourcing this very important part of your business. Outsourcing your page content can prove to be worth every penny of what it will cost.

If you owned a conventional, brick-and-mortar business selling ice cubes, it would be important to have people who needed the ice cubes. I doubt you could sell very many ice cubes in Antarctica, or sand boxes in the desert. My point is, people who are looking on the internet are looking for mainly one thing: information about a specific subject or topic.

Your job as an internet entrepreneur is to provide the exact information being searched for by the type of people you seek for your network marketing business. The type of person for which you are looking is someone who is looking to produce a supplemental income for themselves and their family. They are not just looking for anything that looks good on the surface. The average person is much more informed today than in years past.

They are so burned on hype they can smell a sales pitch a mile away. They do not want to be sold; they want to buy. There is a big difference between the two. To be sold means they have been convinced through powerful advertising or persuasive talk by a salesperson. Many people reject this kind of transaction.

People are looking for information to help them discover a product or service that connects with them on an emotional level, but one in which they can still justify the purchase logically. It is for this reason you must produce strong wordcopy or content that gives them reason to stay on your website and continue reading until they make the decision to purchase from you.

Your use of the internet does not guarantee the success of your network marketing business. If you are not willing to spend time producing persuasive and powerful content for your web pages, you may as well as not have a website at all. Remember, people are looking for information. This is why the internet was created in the first place. People want you to provide them with a reason to buy from you. You provide this reason in the words you place on the pages of your website.

### Drive Traffic to Your Website
### Location, Location, Location

If you lived out in the country and decided to build a convenience store, the most important consideration would be how much business you could draw into your store. This would be determined by how many people lived in your community and the amount of commuters that passed by each day. If you were located in a sparsely populated area you may not have the amount of traffic needed to support your operating expenses.

What it all boils down to is the amount of traffic that comes into your store and how much money they spend before they leave. This same principle applies to your internet presence. Having the most advanced graphics, the flashiest videos, the best products in the world, and the most persuasive written content all means nothing if no one knows you are there.

There are many ways by which to promote the increase of traffic to your website, blog, capture page, or any other web presence. You can call this "trafficking," "trafficology," or "traffication." Just remember, "A rose, by any other name, would smell as sweet." I am sure Shakespeare did not have web traffic in mind when he wrote this, but regardless of what you call it, driving traffic to your web presence is not that complicated.

You could first accomplish this simply through traditional advertising methods. The use of newspaper, radio, TV, and magazine ads can be a powerful tool to direct people to your website. There are always people who are looking for ways to increase their income and help make ends meet. These venues can give you more exposure than you may think. The only drawback to this is the cost associated with traditional advertising. A few seconds on TV can cost thousands of dollars. The same is true for radio. Newspapers and magazines are not as expensive, but still can be cost prohibitive.

Word-of-mouth is certainly a good way to promote your business and website. This method of advertising is always strong because of the credibility factor of people that have integrity telling other people who trust their judgment. This is a very powerful way to get your name out there, but it can work very slowly at times. This method tends to work a little faster in the professional community than in the white-collar or blue-collar demographics.

Business cards, brochures, flyers, and other printed media can draw attention to your website, but the return on your investment in these items can be low. These can be reserved for special events and promotions such as a "Super Saturday" or convention in your local area. There is another consideration for using printed material locally. If you are able to put on an "Income Solution Seminar" in your local area, direct mail campaigns can be effective in drawing the crowd. You would then have the opportunity to direct people to your website once you have built credibility with them.

### Market on the Internet

While you can create a relatively successful marketing campaign using traditional marketing venues, you could never reach the same level of exposure possible as you could when using the internet itself. The internet revolutionized many things in our world, marketing is one of them. A strong internet marketing campaign can yield results never thought possible with traditional marketing.

> A strong internet marketing campaign can yield results never thought possible with traditional marketing.

Now that you know traffic is the key to your business and how to use traditional marketing methods to promote your website, how do you take advantage of the internet as a powerful marketing tool? An internet marketing campaign is a multi-faceted combination of techniques that are geared to increase your presence across several different platforms. These platforms are e-mails, videos, podcasts, social media, capture pages, blogs, banner ads, e-zine articles, and your web page itself. Since you are in control of the marketing for your business, it will be much easier to implement these techniques in a way that is in harmony with your personality and goals.

The first part of this whole process is building a website, capture page, or blog that reflects the purpose and goals for your business. When deciding on the content of the website, keep in mind the importance of power and value when writing your text. This content will make the difference in a visitor's judgment as to whether or not your website is of value. You only get one chance to make this impression. This web presence will be the location to which you will drive traffic.

Websites, capture pages, and blogs are the foundation of your presence on the World Wide Web. In developing these, you must not only ensure you have a high ranking with the major search engines, but you also provide multiple opportunities for people who visit your website to make purchases. The formula for ranking high with the search engines is complex, but not too complicated that you cannot design an effective strategy.

E-mails, videos, podcasts and wordcopy are the internal content of your web presence that delivers your message to those who visit your site as a result of the external content of your marketing methods. Internal and external word copy must be both valuable and relevant to the reader, and must be persuasive enough to lead them through steps of action, bringing them to the eventual purchase of your product or service. This process is called conversion. The conversion rate for your website is measured by calculating the difference between the total number of visitors to your website and the number of visitors who actually make a purchase.

By providing good information, you establish a level of value with people who visit your site. The more valuable you are, the more people will follow you. The more they follow you, the more they will purchase what you have to offer. This process allows you to become the expert and draw an even larger following. This cycle repeats itself until you become the recognized expert and leader of your followers.

### Be Your Virtual Self

There is a relatively new internet networking phenomenon called social media that is quickly becoming the venue of choice for social interaction. There are several different types of social media available on the internet. The most popular are the direct social media outlets such as Facebook, hi5, Twitter, Pounce, and Myspace, just to name a few.

The use of social media for marketing purposes has not gained acceptance among network marketers. This is unfortunate, but will change dramatically over the next few years. This fact gives you the rare opportunity to be ahead of the curve when it comes to internet social marketing. The combination of the internet, social networking, and network marketing is truly a "match made in heaven." For the savvy representative, social media can become a tremendous asset. As people become more educated about social networking and network marketing, the advantages of this union will become more apparent to the participants of both.

Another type of social media is the online personal video platforms like Youtube, Ustream, Stickam, Channelme, and Watchme. These are powerful marketing tools that can add a very personal and professional touch to your business. Many people relate more to a video than to the printed word.

Regardless of the social media platform(s) you choose to use in your business, there are a few important principles to follow. Never use personal social media outlets to only promote your business. It is acceptable to use them for business, but only if the media provides a venue for business promotion. For example, Facebook has "Page," "Group," and "Cause" applications that your business can utilize for promotion. Twitter, because of its design, is almost always used for business promotion. Learn the boundaries and keep them separated.

People are tired of the fake and disingenuous, which is why reality TV is so popular in our culture. They are looking for others who are genuinely interested in them. If you come across as someone who only cares about yourself, forget about being trampled by the moose, you will be "shooting yourself in the foot." When using social media, be yourself. In this crazy world of pretenders, it is refreshing to find people who are genuine. This is actually the draw to Facebook, the largest of the social media outlets where users are able to securely be themselves on the web.

There are people on the internet that will be drawn to you because of your personality. Use your personality to your advantage. Be friendly and participate in the lives of other people. Social media, blogs, and websites are several ways to allow people to see you for who you really are. As others get to know you better, you build the potential to reap more rewards than you ever dreamed possible.

## *Get the Top Spot*

When it comes to doing business on the internet, the goal is to be seen by as many people as possible. Until a website is seen by potential customers, no transactions can take place. Home-based businesses that utilize the internet as a means of promoting their business must gain knowledge and insight into how the process of search engine optimization works. By increasing the volume and improving the quality of traffic to your site you are able to reach larger targeted groups with your message or your product.

When you desire to locate information on the internet, the fastest way to find the appropriate site is through search engines. The role of the search engine is to find websites that contain only the pertinent requested information and produce a list of those websites as a result of the search. The most desirable location (and the most optimal exposure) for your website is on the first page of results produced by the search engines.

Companies that provide these search engines have closely guarded complex algorithms that determine which web sites will be at the top of the search results. These results are based on how well a website meets the criteria of the search. It is these criteria that are closely guarded by the search engine companies.

Part of search engine optimization is the process of editing your website word content and HTML coding so it is relevant to your keywords. This editing is done in attempts to rank as high as possible with the search engines. Search engine optimization (SEO) is an ongoing task and is not an exact science. Entire careers are made in this field. The business owner who maintains a presence on the first few result pages of the search engines, has a much greater chance of having a successful, thriving internet business.

Select carefully who you use for your web page optimization. The right person will help you make your website visible to the masses. One resource for finding good SEO providers is to study the subject from the search engines' web sites. Google has much good information to help you identify the better SEO providers.

### Turn It into Cash

Monetization is the process of converting the many different aspects of your internet based business into income generating opportunities. Many websites use advertising, affiliations and subscriptions to accomplish this goal. The savvy business owner discovers and utilizes as many ways as possible to "monetize" his website. Several of the search engine companies provide information about monetization.

### Target Your Efforts on the Internet

The internet community is growing exponentially. Advertising to a specific geographical area has advantages for someone who wants to focus their internet marketing efforts in only one location. The benefits of geo-targeting are growing more popular as marketing on the internet continues to increase.

### The Name of the Game

Many people hold to the idea that the only way to effectively build a network marketing business is through what is called your "warm market." There are two schools of thought when it comes to warm markets. First, your warm market ends with your circle of influence and, second, your warm market never ends because it continually expands as you help others. It does not matter which school of thought you adopt, because the new warm market is now people who are attracted to you through various social media outlets.

> The new warm market is now people who are attracted to you through various social media outlets.

Other than perseverance, there are two basic essential elements to a successful network marketing business: people and money. Your success is a reflection of how well you draw these two elements to your business and, more specifically, to you. This concept is the missing ingredient so many representatives never learn which can be summed up in one word–Attraction!

This term is used to illustrate a response consumers may have to an on-line advertisement or promotion. When someone finds a promotion that is appealing to them, they are drawn (attracted) to the information and subsequently to the individual offering the information. In traditional marketing, everyone is a prospect. In attraction marketing, only people interested in what you are offering are prospects.

When you hunt for moose, you do not use a duck call. When you send the wrong message, you may attract people who are not interested in your business opportunity. Your message must resonate only with people in your warm market you desire to attract to your business. This is how you attract people that "make a connection" with you and your personality.

We can talk all day about circles of influence, marketing campaigns, personal development, and business opportunities, but they all find their roots in attraction. The absence of attraction in network marketing is like having an airplane with no engine. Attraction is what makes network marketing work. People are attracted to a person, a pay plan, a cause, or all three.

> Your message is the real power of attraction marketing.

Your message is the real power of attraction marketing. There are so many people on the internet, that just a few minutes of exposure for your website can yield a massive response. With proper education and time, you can be incredibly successful, even in a slow economy. The key is knowing the rules of internet and attraction marketing and executing your business choices according those rules.

Attraction marketing is one of the most important elements in a strong marketing program. When you have information people want *and* need, they will be attracted not only to what you have to say, but also to what you have to offer in the way of products, services, business opportunity/income solution, etc.

How do you use this powerful concept of attraction to your advantage in network marketing? Because network marketing is a relationship business, the power of attraction works automatically in the right circumstances. These circumstances are easily created when you put into motion some of the simple marketing techniques listed here in this chapter. You can implement these in your overall strategy whenever you choose; however, you must first understand what these techniques are and how they work.

The following segment is a suggestion of how these techniques can work together to produce a powerful plan of action for your network marketing business. I must point out that this is not designed for only one specific company or business model. You may implement this action plan or a modification of it for any business. This example is based upon the philosophy that attraction is the core of the strategy.

Because this marketing philosophy is based on attraction, there must be an object of attraction that appeals to a broad range of people. The object of attraction for the audience you are trying to reach must be you! This includes your income solution, your website, and the message of your content. They are attracted to what you can do for them. People enjoy spending money because it makes them feel good. As people are attracted to your website and information, they willingly bring their money with them. So, what is the attraction?

For most people, the attraction is the hope of being a better person in some way. This is a fundamental desire for human beings. This is the reason self-help books have always been best sellers. If you break down the motive for people's actions, almost without variation it reveals an internal desire to create a better environment for one's self. The knowledge of this desire is a powerful tool to use in your favor when establishing your marketing strategy.

The first step of this process is to create an appeal for the object to which people are attracted and where people can focus their attention. This technique is used in advertising and the promotion of many different products and services. Certain companies create advertisements with a beautiful woman showcasing the item being advertised. The attraction to the woman is subconsciously associated with the product, creating a desire for the product with the desire for the beauty, and consequently, a desire to purchase.

Since people always desire to better themselves, you will first want to provide information that connects with them on an emotional level that answers their questions, that is relevant to their current circumstances, and that identifies with their experiences. If you are not able to produce powerful content yourself, you can use material written by others or find someone to write it for you. (There are people who sell their writing services for just such occasions.)

Obtaining this information from your website without cost will make them feel they are bettering themselves at no risk. When you supply them with powerful information that addresses their needs, you then become a source of value. The free information portrays you as not only an authority, but as someone who is willing to help others. The value of the information will bring them back for more, and if you over-deliver, they will, more than likely, be willing to pay for it when they return.

The vehicle you will use to convey this information is a web site, blog, or capture page. Each of these has numerous advantages, one of which is that millions of people can see it every day. The information you use must first be content relative to their need or desire and have the ability to "capture" their personal information for follow-up e-mails and correspondence. This page is where you will begin to build their trust in your ability to help them.

Once you have attracted people to you through powerful content, you can then market whatever it is you have to offer. Remember to follow up with them to further discover their desires and needs. If you have properly captured their information, telephone calls and e-mails are often a great way to contact them. Once they show an interest in your income solution, you can follow through and present your business opportunity by inviting them to a presentation meeting, conference calls, or video presentations on the internet.

You must understand the concept of attraction and use the philosophy of drawing people first to yourself, then to your solution, to be successful. Knowing about search engine optimization, social media, websites, or any of the latest and greatest techniques is not what will make your business thrive; it is knowing how to use them properly to attract people to you that will make your business explode.

Just like people do not understand that network marketing is all about the marketing, people do not understand that marketing is first about attraction. You can network all day long, but it is about as effective as throwing mud against the wall to see how much will stick if you do not first attract them to yourself.

### Will Something Viral Make Me Sick?

With a name derived from the way a physical virus spreads (quickly and from person to person), viral marketing has virtually become a household term. The internet perpetuated viral marketing with social networking sites. A message, idea, new product, or event can reach the "viral" stage through conversations via e-mails, in the office lounge, the street corner, through social media, on the telephone, or any other avenue where verbal communication transpires.

Viral marketing can allow you to reach people with your message very quickly. This most often occurs in an online word of mouth form when people "just have to share this with you." The danger of viral marketing is that it can cause your business to grow so rapidly that you are unable to keep up with the demand. This results in negative viral marketing; people visit your website with high expectations and leave disappointed. Word of mouth marketing, as it is often referred to, is one of the most valued tools in marketing. This medium can help a business grow strong and is often employed first with family and friends.

> Viral marketing can allow you to reach people with your message very quickly.

# chapter 20

## summary

*"the round-up"*

## chapter 20

---

# summary

### *"the round-up"*

T he best intentions and the greatest desire to make a difference in your life are worthless if there is no structure to build upon in producing financial freedom. Just as it is important for the coach of a football team to follow the game plan he believes will guide his team to victory, you must follow your game plan, whether it is to simply supplement your income or to gain total financial freedom for you and your family. There are many things you can do that will give you a better chance of winning the financial race, but one thing is for certain: if you do not have a solid plan of action, it will be far more difficult to see the end from the beginning. Having this game plan is what this section is all about.

The following steps are given as a guide for you to follow in designing your game plan that fits your goals and personality. There is not a "one size fits all" plan of action for network marketing businesses. You must take the information you have learned and design your plan based on what works for you. You may have to adjust your plan several times to find the exact combination of methods, techniques, and ideas that produce the desired results.

Very few people start a network marketing business and find extreme success right from the beginning. For the majority, this is a process of discovery that takes several years to perfect. Once you have the right combination, opportunities will present themselves you never before thought possible. The dream of financial and personal freedom is alive and well for those who dare to embrace change and new ideas.

### 1. You must be convinced that the way to financial freedom is through business ownership.

There is an old saying that goes like this: "A man convinced against his will is of the same opinion still." Many people are of the opinion that working for a company is the way to financial freedom or the American dream. Unfortunately for many people today, this dream has turned into a financial nightmare.

Business closings and job layoffs are at an increase, companies that are still operating are struggling to stay afloat, the national debt is the highest ever, and fuel prices continue rising, even after a brief reprieve. And to top it all off, the baby boomers are not leaving the work force as soon as everyone thought, which leaves even fewer jobs for college graduates.

> There is not a "one size fits all" plan of action for network marketing businesses.

These and other factors are changing the way people view their source of income. In the past, people could rely on working for the same company for their entire career. Those days are long gone for the majority of workers. People are realizing the only way to truly find financial security is through becoming a business owner.

Unfortunately, there are still some people that are hanging on to what they think is a "secure" job, thinking the company will be loyal to them after having given the best years of their life to the company. Somehow the words of Tennessee Ernie Ford ring in my head as he sings "Sixteen Tons." I can hear him now, (snap, snap, snap) "You load sixteen tons and what'a ya get, another day older and deeper in debt, St. Peter don't ya call me cause I can't go, I owe my soul to the company store."

If I had not experienced the loyalty to a company and subsequent job loss in a downsizing, I might not understand this either, but the fact is that there are many people who know the exact feeling after having lost their job. One thing I came to realize soon after losing this job was that you cannot be loyal to a non-entity. What is a company? It is not a person; it is the sum total of all its parts. It is a non-entity.

Once you realize you cannot be loyal to a non-entity, you also realize this same non-entity cannot be loyal to you either. Many people struggle with this concept. They believe they should receive something for so many years of loyal service. The truth is, a company owes nothing to its employees beyond payment for hours traded. Anything a company offers an employee above a payroll check is a perk.

As an employee, hours of labor are traded for the company's money. An employee can only earn so much money because there are only so many hours in a day. No matter how much money an employee wants to make, no matter how badly a person wants to be financially free, it is nearly impossible to do so while producing a profit for someone else.

For you to understand the principles of wealth building, you must realize the fallacy of gaining financial freedom as an employee. This is not an attempt to convince you of this principle because you must convince yourself of this truth. There must be a fundamental shift in your understanding for you to be completely convinced that the only way to financial freedom is through owning a business. This must be the core belief of the network marketer. Without this belief, there will not be enough motivation to continue when things get tough.

## 2. You must believe that network marketing is the right business vehicle for you.

One of the most successful, and arguably the most talented, basketball players in history is Michael Jordan. Although he never held the record for points scored in a game, he was known as the world's greatest clutch player in basketball. A lesser known fact about Michael Jordan is that his first love of sports was for baseball.

He actually played for the Birmingham Barons and was considered to be a less-than-average player by many. A personal quote of Michael

Jordan is, "If you're trying to achieve, there will be roadblocks. I've had them; everybody has had them. But obstacles don't have to stop you. If you run into a wall, don't turn around and give up. Figure out how to climb it, go through it, or work around it."

Network marketing may be considered by many to be their second choice of income solutions. If Michael Jordan's story is of any consequence, it would be to make this exact point. Many people have a plan "A" that does not give them what they dreamed of when they finished college or started their life-long career. There is no shame in this whatsoever. The shame would be to continue down the same path with no regard to where it is taking them.

> For you to understand the principles of wealth building, you must realize the fallacy of gaining financial freedom as an employee.

In your life, there may be dreams you once had of becoming financially free, but over time that dream slipped away into obscurity. Network marketing is the basketball instead of the baseball for many people. If Michael Jordan had continued playing baseball, he would, without a doubt, not be worth in excess of 400 million dollars right now. He had to make a decision about which vehicle would take him to where he dreamed of being. That vehicle turned out to be basketball instead of baseball.

Your career may be as a professional person such as a doctor, attorney, architect, teacher, politician, or entertainer, but you must ask yourself the question, "When you are not working, are you getting paid?" Unless you have a contract with Nike, like Michael Jordan, you probably do not have another source of income. A recent conversation with a friend of mine in the medical field stated that it was becoming increasingly difficult to meet the requirements of the insurance companies.

This trend seems to be getting worse, not better. If forced into early retirement, would you have the financial resources available to continue your present lifestyle? This is a valid question, one that many professionals are asking themselves everyday. If your answer is "no", making the decision to start "plan B" would be wise.

What is your plan B going to be? Would you start another practice or open another office in the same field or profession? I seriously doubt it. Network marketing is one, if not the best, way to produce a substantial income in a relatively short amount of time.

As a professional, you probably have a fairly large circle of influence already. This influence can be leveraged to build a business that allows you not only to continue your current lifestyle, but also to be free to choose how you use your time, money, and talents. For this to happen, you must be convinced that network marketing is the right vehicle for you. Network marketing is only a means to an end, but it is a very good one. If baseball isn't working for you, perhaps you should try basketball!

### 3. Find the company that will provide the income solution that fits you best.

When searching for the right combination of characteristics in a company, more than likely it will be a one that carries the products and services you can be passionate about and that has a balanced and lucrative pay structure that attracts you. Making these determinations can take time. Do not be afraid to take the time necessary to research these characteristics before you decide which is best for you.

The most important consideration when deciding which company is right for you is a company that has a good pay structure. This may be more difficult than you might think. Most network marketing companies claim to have the best pay structure in the industry. You should look for a company that gives regular pay increases to the representatives over the life of the company.

A tell-tale sign of how well the company is performing in this area is whether or not the company is actually giving pay increases to its representatives or reducing the pay incentives. A company that has the representatives' success at the heart of its pay structure does all it can to consistently increase the amount of the payouts to the representatives. This pay structure should include both residual commission and bonus pay incentives.

Bonus pay is exactly that, a bonus. Bonus pay should not be the only element of the pay structure. Residual income is a far more important element. Residual income is when you make a sale one time, yet you continue receiving an income from that transaction every month the bill is paid. Residual income is one of the most powerful wealth-building tools available.

Many companies are aware of this extremely powerful revenue tool. Consider the electric company from which you receive your electricity. You call them to begin service at your residence and they come out and place a power meter on the side of your house one time, yet they continue receiving revenue from that meter every month you make a payment. Insurance companies have used the power of residual income for many years. You sign up for a premium one time, but make monthly payments. Banks and lending institutions also use this principle of wealth building to the fullest degree.

> With network marketing, everyone is on a level playing field.

How about your cell phone service? Did you know that when you go to a store, such as Wal-Mart, Radio Shack, Best Buy, Target, the kiosk at the mall, or any other outlet where you can purchase cell phone service, once you sign the contract for the service, the location where you initiated the contract receives a commission every time you pay your bill. These companies know the power of residual income very well. This is why they carry products such as cell phones and satellite cable TV service.

If you could become a representative for a company that allows you to be the middle-man between these companies and their customers, like Wal-Mart, Radio Shack and others do, you can amass a very substantial revenue stream from the residual income alone. Residual income can take a long time to build. It is the bonus structure that allows you to receive immediate reward for your efforts, while the residual income steadily builds over time. If you were to locate a company that provided a well-balanced pay structure utilizing both these qualities, you would have found the proverbial "leprechaun's pot of gold," or the "goose that laid the golden egg"

Another consideration is the manner in which a person acquires and continues in each level of promotion. The better companies offer position promotions that are not removed if quotas are not met. In other words, the absence of quotas to remain at a given level is a very attractive characteristic.

Not all companies are able to accommodate this requirement due to their particular business model. This does not mean they are not worthy of consideration, but you must consider this very carefully before making your decision. In some companies, if you are promoted to a new level and have a bad month, as often happens, you may be penalized for it.

The amount of initial investment should also have some bearing in your decision. The advantage of almost all network marketing companies is they have a very low initial cost to get started. The benefit is obvious. You have the potential for a substantial income with a very low up-front investment. This is much different than traditional brick-and-mortar businesses that require large sums of money to become operational.

For the average person, even buying a franchise is cost prohibitive in most cases. With network marketing, everyone is on a level playing field. The average person has the same opportunity as everyone else in the business. When considering an opportunity, most people want to know basically three things:

1. How much does it cost to join?

2. What do I have to do?

3. How much do I get paid?

If you can find the answers to these basic questions, and you are satisfied with the answers given by the company, then perhaps you have found the company that is right for you.

### 4. Join the company.

This may seem a bit simplistic, but it is a very important step. Many people will get analysis paralysis and never make the decision to break out of the mold they have been poured into week after week and year after year as an employee. The dentist in the first chapter may have been in danger after he fired the first shot at the moose, but had he not taken the first step of going on the hunt, he would not have the trophy hanging on his wall even now. Sometimes we must risk everything to have everything.

"Nothing ventured, nothing gained." Many self-made millionaires lost everything, several times, before finally reaching their goal.

In network marketing there is actually little to lose, perhaps a few hundred dollars in initial investment, a few hours of time, and a little pride. But, what is this compared to what can be gained? The opportunity to produce a substantial income, on a part time basis, is not found in many other industries.

The key is to get started right away. All the best equipment in the world, the most thorough preparation, the best laid plans, and the greatest of intentions would not have produced the victory the dentist enjoyed and the pride of such an accomplishment, if he had not actually gone to Alaska. The most favorable trip is no trip at all until it is actually taken. The glory is in the doing, not in the knowing or even in having done.

## 5. Become the expert in network marketing.

Becoming the expert in network marketing does not mean you must know every detail of every network marketing company in history. Becoming the expert is learning everything you can about your chosen company and how to help others become successful in their business. You may ask yourself why it is important to be an expert. Network marketing allows average people to have above average incomes for themselves, but the only way to accomplish this is by helping others become successful. There is not a shortcut to this process.

For you to help others in this way, you must be knowledgeable and capable of transferring that knowledge to other people. You become an expert by choosing to engage in personal development. We have talked at length in previous chapters about the necessity of personal development.

The natural progression of personal development is teaching others and helping them succeed in their business by duplicating yourself through their actions. Once they have become the expert, they will continue this process in their organization. This process continues through all the levels of your business, strengthening your business and increasing your income as a result.

### 6. Implement what you have learned.

When I was in high school, I played several sports. My favorite was baseball, but when baseball was not in season I also loved wrestling, basketball and soccer. I excelled in wrestling, winning the unlimited class championship my senior year. Although I was slightly taller for my age, I recall not enjoying basketball as much, but one thing I remember very well was the plays we would run over and over again in practice.

We ran these plays so many times we could run them in our sleep. When it came time to compete against rival teams, we knew the plays so well they went like clockwork. We were regional champions for several years running. I will always attribute our winning to the practices we were made to endure. We would never have been regional champions had we not implemented on the court for game day what we had learned off the court in practice.

You must also apply this same principle to your network marketing business. Regardless of how much you learn, there comes a time to implement the things you have been taught. Consider the first few months in your business as practice by using this book to develop your game plan. When you learn what you need to win the financial freedom game, implement your plan with all the excitement and enthusiasm you can muster. Do not let the shouts from the opposing team discourage you. Stick to the plays you have developed, stay for the whole game, and you will be a winner.

### 7. Don't Quit!

Most statistics show that approximately 90% of direct sales representatives quit, and yet the majority of people in America today consider themselves to be above average. A large number of representatives give up on their business, walking away from an amazing opportunity. Those who are dedicated to their business stand a greater chance of producing an extraordinary income as a network marketing business owner.

If you research and study many of the extremely wealthy in our country, you will find they overcame failure and overwhelming odds to succeed. They caught a vision of something, pursued it and did not give up or quit even after their success. Take to heart their perseverance; push on just one more minute, one more mile, one more month. Don't Quit!

Just because Wall Street crashes does not mean those of us left on Main Street have to follow suit. Taxes may go up, inflation may rise, and our government may make decisions with which we do not agree. But we, as Americans, though these things may affect our economy, do not have to let them affect our bottom line. We are still Americans, and we still have the freedom and the right to choose our destiny and to follow our dreams.

The average person in America today is afraid of the economy, but there is no reason to fear if you are prepared for it. Just like the dentist had the guide to show him where the moose was in the woods, you should have a guide to help you not only survive this economy, but to thrive in it. By now you know and understand that the future belongs to those who prepare for it and take action.

> Network marketing is one of the last bastions of capitalism available to the average American.

Network marketing is one of the last bastions of capitalism available to the average American. Network marketing is not about seeing who can make the most money. Network marketing is about making a difference in your life and in the lives of others. It is about giving back and building a business on the premise of giving first in order to receive. It is about freedom, and taking charge of your life; owning your time instead of selling it to a boss or a company for the reward of a plaque and a watch in thirty years. Network marketing is about owning your business and building a source of income that will continue even when you retire.

There is a logical sequence of events that a person will go through to find financial freedom. If you can learn that sequence and determine where you are in that order of events, knowing what you now know, you will be able to help not only yourself, but multitudes of other people; securing not only your financial future but possibly even that of your children, grandchildren, and great grandchildren. What a legacy for you to be remembered as the person who helped so many reach their goals and dreams, and in doing so, made your family wealthy for generations.

There is a door of opportunity available to those who are willing to walk through it. If you would like to learn more and are ready to start your journey today, visit **www.mooseconomy.com**.

# appendix i

# mark burgess

In the spring of 1992, my wife and I were introduced to the world of network marketing. We lived in our home state of South Carolina. Several years earlier we had lived in Dallas, TX for a couple of years while I was in college. Friends of ours who still lived in the Dallas area invited us to meet them halfway between South Carolina and Texas. They had "something" they wanted to share with us that was going to make them wealthy. Of course, we were very interested to hear what they had to say.

For weeks before we left for the trip, I tried to get them to reveal to us what the "something" was, but they would not budge. We even jokingly threatened not to make the trip if they would not tell us. They called our bluff, and still, not a word from them as to what it was. I even mentioned a well-known network marketing company's name, and said I was definitely not interested if that's what it was.

Even at this, they would not reveal what it was. There was so much anticipation as to what this amazing "something" was that they had found. Little did I know, this expectancy was exactly what they wanted. They had built up this mystery in our minds so much that we didn't stand a chance when it came time to reveal it to us. So we made the trip to meet with them. We enjoyed the chance to get away for a few days and spend some time together.

When we finally arrived at the predetermined location, we spent the better part of the day (actually through two meal times) at a restaurant catching up and viewing diagrams, circles, and boxes of various types. The information they gave us made perfect sense. This really seemed to be the greatest opportunity to reach our financial dreams that we had ever seen in our lifetime. They told us about their goal of owning and running a Dude Ranch for kids, and how this business was going to help them accomplish those dreams. At the end of the presentation they finally told us the name of the company.

I know the color must have drained from our faces. We could not have been more shocked. It was exactly the company that we had told them we did not want anything to do with. I realize now, we did not know what we thought we knew about the company.

The business plan they showed us was very believable. We had based our previous opinions on things we heard from others who had been in the same business. There were stories of how people lost their homes and spent fortunes just trying to maintain a certain position in the company. There was also the story about having a garage full of product that could never be reduced short of throwing it away. Of course, many of these stories tended to be exaggerated, depending on how angry or unsuccessful the person telling the story happened to be.

We did not blame our friends or get upset with them. We enjoyed taking the trip and catching up with them. We also realized, through that experience, that there were more ways to produce an income than just working for someone else. This was a turning point in our lives concerning the network marketing industry.

Prior to this meeting, we had not been accurately informed about network marketing, nor did we have any exposure to industry. So it was beneficial to us in this regard. We began to see how this type of business could allow people to live anywhere they wanted, work their business from home, and enjoy freedoms only wealth can and does provide.

We were young at the time, in our mid-twenties, and had dreams of being financially free. We had not had the "lucky breaks" that other people we knew were enjoying. We had a good work ethic and the character to follow through with perseverance. However, we also knew that if we were going to experience financial success, we were going to need a special opportunity that would allow us to realize our dreams. This kind of thinking set us up for more disappointments than you can imagine. While we were willing to work very hard at whatever job we had, we did not have the understanding of basic principles that would allow us to successfully navigate the ocean of the fiscal world.

Instead of taking sound financial steps to ensure our future, we started looking for the "silver bullet" that would remove our monetary problems and set us up for a life of pecuniary ease. Since we had now been exposed to another way to make money, we were not afraid of launching out into the deep.

I had previously owned a small contracting business when my wife and I were first married, so we were more than willing to start a business from scratch and fund it with every paycheck we received from our regular job...and we did just that. We sacrificed many things until we finally reached the breaking point where there was no more to sacrifice. I worked at this business for a few years, until the housing market forced me to find employment at a grocery store, stocking shelves at night.

As we sat across from the table with our friends and started dreaming about what we could accomplish through a business like this, they must have recognized the "wheels turning" in our heads and suggested that we go with them to look at motor homes. (I guess if you're going to dream, you might as well dream big.) So off we went to a place that sold motor homes and campers. I suppose buying a new motor home, being a symbol of success, was an idea they were trying to share with us. When we finished looking at the motor homes we said our good-byes, took a few pictures, and went our separate ways.

This meeting was a turning point for us. Although I did not want anything to do with this particular company, our conversation and the information they gave us opened our eyes to a life that was possible through network marketing. For the first time we realized our potential to have personal financial freedom.

For the next couple of days, as we traveled home to South Carolina, all we talked about were the possibilities now open to us. If we could only find the right company that had the right product, we would be set. This began a journey for us that lasted the next decade. We started looking for the perfect "vehicle" that would carry us to the life of financial freedom we were looking for.

We became involved with one network marketing company after another, spending much more money than we made, just trying to succeed in this new industry we had discovered. We worked hard with each company. We went to all the meetings and told all our friends and family members about this wonderful product and opportunity we were offering. I know they got tired of hearing about the next great thing that came along, but they supported us anyway.

I distinctly remember one company for which we sold water filters and air purifiers. These were not bad products, just overpriced. Many times my wife and I would walk out of a family's home with a check in our hands for several hundred dollars, and feel bad because we knew they could not really afford to make the purchase.

Because we had done such a good job of "selling" the product, they bought it. It did have health benefits, of course, but we could not overcome the feeling that we were taking advantage of them somehow. Needless to say we did not last long in that business.

Although we did not continue with that company, we did pursue other opportunities over the next several years. We worked with companies that provided everything from long-distance telephone service, internet storefronts, travel, and prepaid legal services to household products. You name it, we tried it. Many years and many disappointments later, the "straw that broke the camel's back" was when we lost over six thousand dollars in a company that did not represent things in an honest way.

At this time in our lives, my wife and I had invested and lost a great deal of money trying to get one network marketing business after another off the ground. We could not figure out why things had not gone the way our up-lines had told us they would go. We were so despondent that we dropped out of the industry altogether.

We were tired and frustrated, and felt as if we had been used as pawns to make other people wealthy. We did not realize this was exactly what was happening in our "regular" jobs. Our experiences created an extreme skepticism and distrust for any business remotely connected with network marketing.

Over the next few years, my wife and I worked very hard at our traditional jobs. We had been promoted to middle management and had resigned ourselves to the thought that the only way to reach the "American Dream" was through working for someone else and being promoted up the corporate ladder. We had excellent credit and could purchase anything we desired. Eventually, we bought some land and built our dream home.

Many years later, time dictated change and, as a result, I had to find a part time job in order to make ends meet. I started working various part-time jobs in new home construction, custom cabinet building, and home remodeling. These jobs met our needs for short periods of time, but I needed something steadier. This is where network marketing came back into focus for us once again.

While working these different part time jobs, my oldest brother kept telling me about this "opportunity" he had ran across. He had never been a network marketing type of person. In fact, he was, and still is, working with the same company for twenty seven years. I was so skeptical about network marketing "opportunities" that I felt almost sick just thinking about getting involved with another company. Yet my brother persisted, and I listened to him for over seven months before even looking at what he wanted to show me.

I gave him every excuse in the book. Many times he would call me on his way to work in the mornings and I would ignore his calls. Other times I told him I was in the middle of a book project, and I did not have time. Because I was traveling out of state on occasion, I even used traveling as an excuse. When I finally finished the first book in a series on which I was working, I had no more excuses.

A friend and I were sitting at his dining room table having a discussion about income solutions when we decided to "just take a look" at the "opportunity" my brother was telling me about. We went on-line to watch a video produced by this company. We watched the presentation, and what we saw simply amazed us. At the end of the presentation, which lasted only about twenty minutes, we both concluded that this was the greatest opportunity to build personal wealth we had ever seen.

I called my brother immediately and asked him if he could be at my house (200 miles away) that coming Saturday. He agreed to come and we had twelve people at our home to hear the presentation. I and my friend joined the business within the next few days. Ten out of the twelve people that were in my living room that Saturday also joined the business with us. We were so excited to see this kind of response and started receiving paychecks just as they said.

Our paychecks were increasing and we felt really good about the choice we had made to get involved with yet another network marketing "opportunity" after all these years. A few months into the business, we were told that our business was growing much faster than some others. My brother had been in the business less than a year, and he was already seeing monthly incomes in excess of fifteen thousand dollars.

This was indeed a very different company from what we had experienced in the past. My wife and I had the privilege of meeting and participating in a private dinner with the founder of the company after having been in the company for only a few weeks. We were told that we had been given the opportunity to get involved with a company that was still in its infancy. This also was much different than the other companies we had worked in.

We worked very hard at our new business. For the first time we had actually learned what network marketing was all about. We realized the difference between this company and the others we had been involved with in the past. We believed strongly in the company's vision and had grown to admire the founder for his integrity, openness, generosity, and genuine manner in which he dealt with everyone.

We knew this company was different because he was different. After a couple of months in the business we had actually won a promotion that allowed us the opportunity to spend a couple of days visiting the home office, touring the facilities, participating in special meetings and meals with the founder and top staff of the company, and attending a professional baseball game, all at the company's expense.

I attended every training session and convention I could. I participated in every conference call available and was given a free conference call time slot to use for helping our down-line grow their business. I spent hundreds of dollars on company material to give to prospects and new reps. I downloaded all the forms and information that was available from the company web site.

I spent hours studying the different products, services, and company policies and procedures. I put together "Welcome" folders for new representatives and gave them to everyone I personally sponsored so they could get a jump start on their business while they waited for the material from the company to arrive. I could not do too much!

My friend and I spent hours a day brainstorming and developing strategies on how we were going to "crack" the city in which we lived. I developed and printed invitation cards we would pass out to people we came in contact with, to invite them to our weekly meetings.

This was going to be our vehicle to financial freedom. We were so dedicated to seeing this through to the end that we did not see many of the things that we had forgotten about many years earlier. I had a list of over five hundred people that I diligently and methodically contacted. I spent weeks at a time away from my family trying to engage my warm market. I obtained lists from friends that I contacted hoping to find those "nuggets," as they say. I used the "three foot rule," then expanded it to thirty feet, then three hundred miles.

As time went on, my business started to slow down. Each month that passed became more and more difficult to find people interested in what I had to offer. Not only was I having a tough time at it, so were many people in our down-line. My up-line encouraged us to keep going and not quit; they were seeing a slow down as well. I did not intend to quit. I still have not quit to this day, but something had definitely happened. In spite of how hard I worked and how many meetings I conducted, there was just not enough response.

Naturally, our income also started to decline. Our goal from the beginning was for the business to pay for itself, and it has many times over, but still the slow down occurred. I came to believe the problem was not with us. I did not know exactly why, but I knew we were doing everything right. Our excitement was high, and it showed in our meetings. It did not matter that things had slowed down. We were going to see this thing through no matter what. This was our vehicle of choice to become financially free.

Little did I know at the time, there are many thousands of people who have experienced exactly the same thing. What was the problem? Why were we in a similar place we found ourselves many years earlier? I really thought things were going to be much different this time. Was it just me? Did I not have what it takes? These are the questions thousands of people ask themselves every day. It is well known that over 90% of those who begin working in network marketing quit after only a few months in their business. I was determined not to be one of these people (again).

I started researching and reading anything and everything I could get my hands on. I spent hours at the computer researching the network marketing industry. I spent tons of money on books dealing with the subject. I ordered books online, frequented the used book stores to find deals, and purchased new books until I amassed a good library of just network marketing and motivational books. I attended seminars and training courses and bought CD's and DVD's. I decided I was not going to let this go, as I had done in the past. What I have discovered, and what I want to share with you is very important, and enlightening.

The problem was me! How is that for a shocker? What I failed to realize all those years was, "It's not about the products; it's about marketing!" It doesn't matter how good (or bad) your product is. It is how you market your product that counts. You can have the greatest product in the world and never make a dime if no one knows about it. You can have the worst product in the world and still make a lot of money if you market it properly.

You can also have the greatest opportunity in the world, and never make a penny, if no one knows about it. It is all about your circle of influence and how many people you can get in front of your information. This fact cannot be disputed.

There are many thousands of people who have tried and quit some network marketing business. This does not mean network marketing is bad. It simply means it is not understood. The attrition rate for many network marketing companies is around 90%. This is a staggering number considering the growth of the industry and the income potential.

As people in our organization began to experience a struggle in their businesses, we decided to produce a compilation of information, techniques, suggestions, methods, tools, and concepts we felt would strengthen them in several areas of their business.

"It is not impossibilities which fill us with the deepest despair, but possibilities which we have failed to realize" - Robert Mallett, 1915-

The network marketing industry is no different from any other industry that seeks to exist in good times as well as the bad. A downturn in the economy always causes a mass movement toward alternative sources of income. The network marketing industry does well when the nation's economy is on a downward trend. No one wishes for this, but, for the person who recognizes it, this environment is a great open door of opportunity.

People still have goals and dreams and are willing to work very hard to accomplish them. Network marketing is one of the most honorable and ethical ways to make a living; however, it is not an easy business in which to work. There are many skeptics and critics of this industry. People always criticize that which they either do not understand or that of which they are afraid.

Even though network marketing has been around for many years, it is the wave of the future. Do your research and you will discover this truth for yourself.

– GMB

# appendix ii

# keith henschen

I grew up on a dairy farm in the Midwest. I learned early that farming is not the business of choice for building wealth. It is, on the other hand, a great business for those who are self sufficient, hard working, and able to figure things out for themselves.

For instance, I can remember many times working on the tractors and implements because it was too expensive to send them to the mechanic. We would often fabricate things to make our job easier. We built and maintained the barns and buildings. All this was done while maintaining the herd, milking twice a day, and planting or harvesting crops.

Farming of any sort is not for the faint of heart. Though farming may not be the best way to become wealthy, it is one of the most rewarding jobs. It teaches a great deal of discipline and affords a wonderful quality of life. Many of my fondest memories are from working on the farm.

When I graduated from high school, I decided to go to college. I held several different jobs throughout my college career. Usually, I would change jobs at the beginning of a school year or between semesters. On more than one occasion, after working for a week or so the boss told me I was the hardest working person or best worker he had ever employed.

This was not because I went to work every day with the goal of becoming the boss's pet. I simply went to work and employed the principles I had learned by working on the farm. When I got to work, it was time to work. I had the mind-set to get the job done while other employees were there only to draw a paycheck.

My work ethic quickly started to pay off. I saw pay raises and promotions to better positions while others would either quit or stall in their positions. As my superiors saw my drive and desire to work, they would entrust me with more responsibilities. Accepting these responsibilities, I would learn new skills and also learn how to handle the pressures that came with them.

I can remember becoming frustrated with the laziness and apathy of many of the employees. I began to think like my employer. I started watching people and noticing the positive and negative qualities they possessed. I began to see things from a different vantage point.

As an employee, we often see only one side of the coin, and that is the boss requires a certain number of hours per week and a certain task to be done in that period of time, whereas an employer is looking at the other side of the coin and sees how much product needs to go out the door by a certain time in order to make a profit. Not only that, but he is also thinking about the overhead of the building, the employees, the insurance, the inventory, and the list goes on.

When I finished my college career, I worked for two different men who were business owners. They taught me a great deal about the business I was interested in and about how to run a business. I learned from them the importance of good record keeping, and that there is a cost of doing business, but if you are unwilling to satisfy those costs, you will not last long in the business world.

These men were so gracious and willing to be transparent with me in their business showing me how to use leverage. I learned I could leverage my time by employing others, getting more done with people working for me than I could ever do by doing the job by myself. I also found that I could leverage my money in several different ways.

I could leverage my money by purchasing my materials at wholesale and selling the finished product at a retail price. I could also continue to leverage my money by investing my profits into a number of different places where I could earn interest and make my money work for me.

At first, I just started taking odd jobs, gaining the experience and confidence I needed to grow my business. Soon, I went full time in my business, and, before long, I was able to provide employment opportunities for others. I continued to work my business this way until I realized I could grow my business faster if I specialized in one area.

Until this point, my business required a broad knowledge coupled with a great number of skills and tools at any given time. When I realized I could and should specialize, it actually came as a great relief to me. I was now able to become very proficient and efficient at doing that one type of work. Another perk to this new business direction was the fact that it was something that I really loved doing. I was passionate about it and it was clear to others that I truly loved what I was doing.

As my business changed, I went through the struggles of finding the new clients that needed and wanted my services. Since my menu of services had been narrowed, the number of current clients who now wanted what I had to offer reflected the same. It was like a buffet style restaurant doing away with the buffet and serving only high end steaks and seafood. Along with the change of menu comes a change in the patronage.

So here I was, looking at this great new business and not knowing exactly how to find those who needed what I had. I studied and learned about my field, I subscribed to periodicals about it, and even took some classes to hone my skills.

As I worked my business, I was constantly searching for more customers, always asking for more referrals, always making phone calls and setting meetings to show prospective customers. I soon found I was working just as hard to find new customers as I was to fill the orders I currently had generated. But I knew if I did not continuously find more people wanting my products and services, my business would soon run out and I would be without a job.

It seemed as though I became fixed in a vicious cycle of prospecting, producing, and projecting. I very quickly came to the conclusion that there had to be a better way: a way of bringing people to me so I did not have to hunt for them. I contacted the local yellow pages about listing in the phone book for the year (too expensive up front for my small business).

I put up a website, and made some attractive brochures and set them out at local businesses. I focused on networking with others who were in businesses that would regularly need my services. My web site did nothing for me because there was no traffic to the site. The brochures were not as profitable as I had planned for them to be.

I continued to do what I could to market my business, and soon there were enough orders coming in that things really started moving. For the following several years my business literally doubled in annual revenues. I increased my yearly goals and before I knew it I was aiming for the moon.

Around the middle of the second year in my business, one of my good friends introduced me to a business that helps people to manage money and get out of debt. This was a fledgling company with good morals, high standards and a mission of truly helping people. He told me about the company and asked me if I would be interested in working with him.

Considering the fact that I wanted to learn more about money, I agreed to take a look at what he had to offer. I went to the office and met with the owner of the business. He shared with me his goal to change the way the majority of Americans handle their money. He showed me some major flaws in the practices of the average consumer and how to remedy many common financial problems. He had a plan of how he could influence a small number of people and then use their influence to touch the lives of a greater number of people who then would turn around and influence even more and more. Before you know it nearly everyone would know about this man and his business and would have a chance to be helped by it.

I thought this was great in and of itself. I have always had a great desire to help people any way I could and here was a great opportunity to do so. But there was more. Not only could I help people in this business but I could actually get paid to do so. I could make money by teaching people how to save theirs.

This was the best of both worlds. It was also my introduction to network marketing. I soon learned what a downline and a compensation plan was. I learned that I could teach others to do what I was doing and in turn earn a little from them doing the same thing I was doing. This all made sense to me because I was able to do what I had previously learned from my two mentors in business. I could leverage my time with people working with me in my downline.

Shortly after joining that business on a part time basis I read a book by Robert Kiyosaki called "The Cash-flow Quadrant." In the book, he talks about the four different types of money earners. He names them as the E, S, B and I quadrants, each portraying a different type of person. The "E" quadrant stands for the Employees. These people comprise over ninety percent of the population and are known to depend on the security of their jobs. They live every week from paycheck to paycheck and are willing to accept less in return for the feeling of security in their jobs.

Very close in description to these people are those who make up the "S" quadrant. Self employed men and women are a step away from the security of the "job" into the security of self reliance and depending on their strength and grit to earn their way to financial freedom. They are known as the ones who get tired of being dragged down by those around them in the work place. They can do a better job than anyone in their field. There is a great niche for these kinds of people in our world today.

Next, Kiyosaki described the "B" quadrant as the Business Owners in America today. By saying "Business Owners," he was talking about those who employed a great number of people. These people thrive on a thing called freedom. They are driven by the dream of someday not having to work to earn a living but to retire young and live their lives the way they choose. The thing he said about this group is that they are a smaller group of people who are willing to take greater risks because they understand the value of leverage. They are known for winning big and losing big. This group is not for the faint of heart.

Finally he described the last group, the "I" quadrant – Investors. This is the smallest group of income earners in America. They invest their money into different things, whether in the stock market or in other businesses. They take the greatest risks and are also driven by their drive for freedom.

This was revolutionary to me. I had never heard anything like this before, yet it all made such perfect sense. I had never before stepped back and look at my life, placed a finger on where I was financially, and identified where I wanted to be. It was as if I had found the legend to my road map and now I knew where I was headed.

When I was confronted with the opportunity to join the company with which I am now involved, my first response was that this sounds almost too good to be true. I owned my business, I was making it, and my business was what I would consider to be successful. But, because of the economy, I knew harder times were on the horizon. I was not sure if my current business plan was going to survive the coming onslaught. I changed my marketing strategy and kept my eyes open for other avenues.

I studied business methods and strategies, soaking up all the information I could about money and how to get it. I studied everything I could to ensure the success of my small business, and yet I started to see my sales fall and the phone stop ringing. As this happened, I first started asking other business men and women how their business was doing. The initial response I received was something like "oh we are doing great," or "I've heard others are struggling but we are still doing fine." The longer I continued to ask, the more the answers changed.

More and more businesses were struggling and more and more businesses were closing their doors. When the opportunity came along, I had to ask myself a few questions. Is it possible for me to succeed at a new thing in the midst of a slowing economy? Is this just another scam that is coming down the pike? Can I afford to take a few hundred dollar risk? Can I afford not to?

I stepped out by faith and made the commitment to myself, my wife and my family that I would do my best with this new opportunity. As I began my business, things started off very well. I made my first promotion in the business in a fairly short period of time and have seen my business produce far more revenue for me than it ever cost.

There have been tough times and a multitude of difficulties that I have had to overcome. The one thing I have learned is this: Never Quit! Do not give up! It is those who continue in network marketing who work their way to the top. Granted, the road is easier for some than it is for others, but those who pay no attention to negative influences but continue working their business will eventually win.

Too many people think network marketing is a microwave business: they want the instant results without the work. Some people have the misconception that network marketing is an easy business. They begin their business with the idea that everyone will see what they see and that things will just explode and they will be rich in a matter of months. What you must understand is that network marketing is not easy, but it is simple. If you can master the simplicity, use the right tools and help others do the same. You too may see measures of success beyond your wildest imagination.

– KSH

# index